WORSHIP TOGETHER.com®
EVERLASTINGGOD
25 MODERN WORSHIP FAVORITES

T0082962

ISBN 978-1-4234-5935-4

HAL•LEONARD®
CORPORATION

7777 W. BLUEMOUND RD. P.O. BOX 13819 MILWAUKEE, WI 53213

Visit Hal Leonard Online at
www.halleonard.com

BEAUTIFUL ONE

Words and Music by
TIM HUGHES

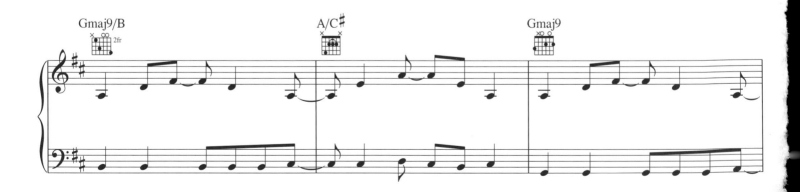

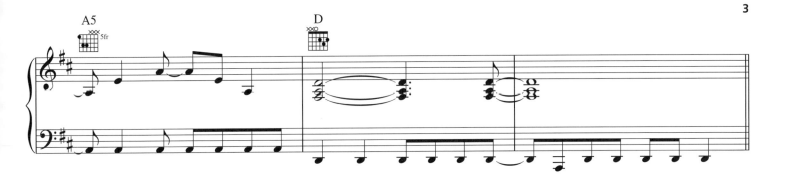

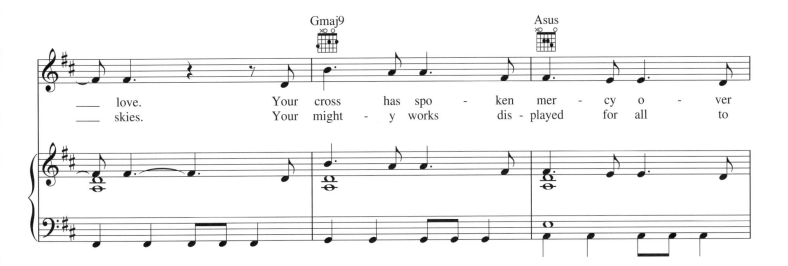

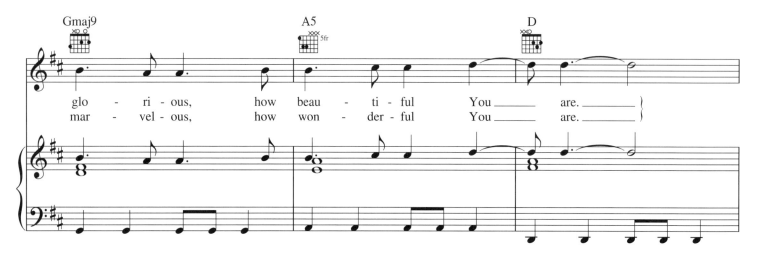

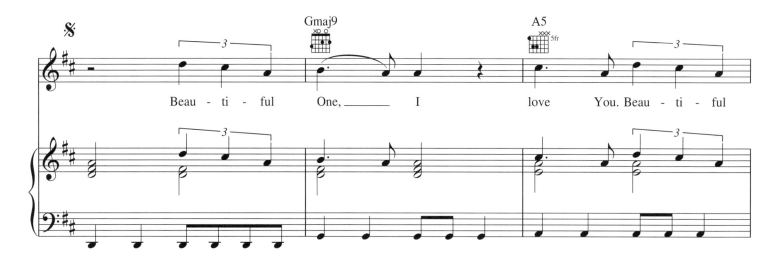

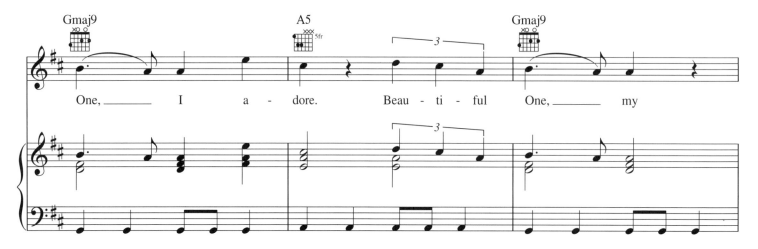

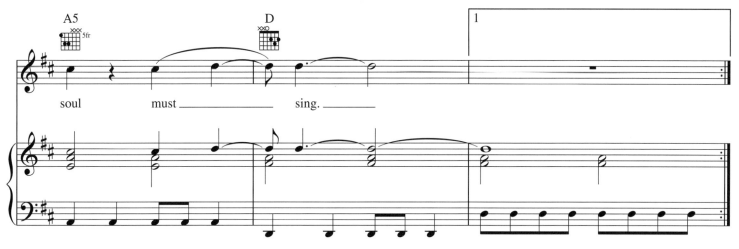

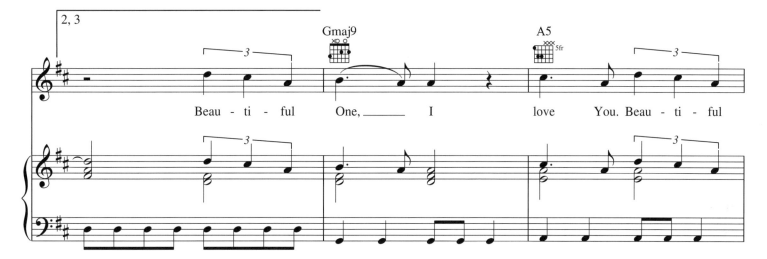

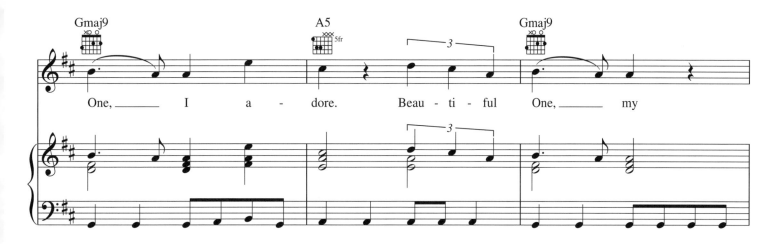

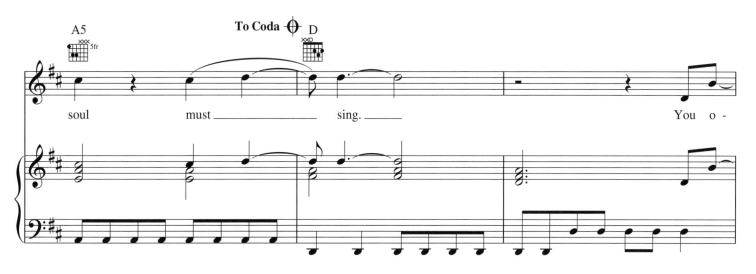

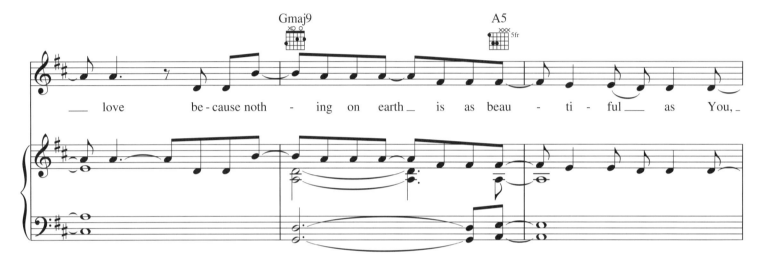

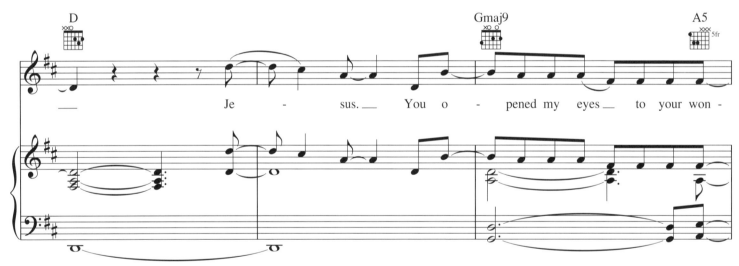

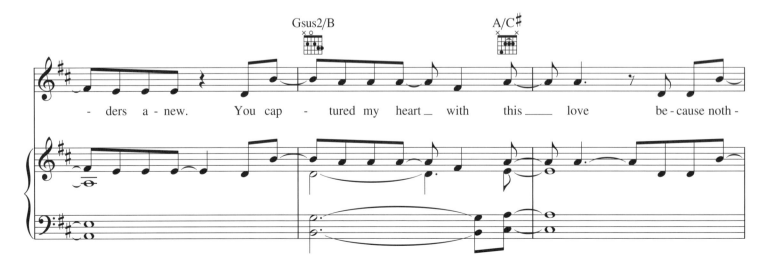

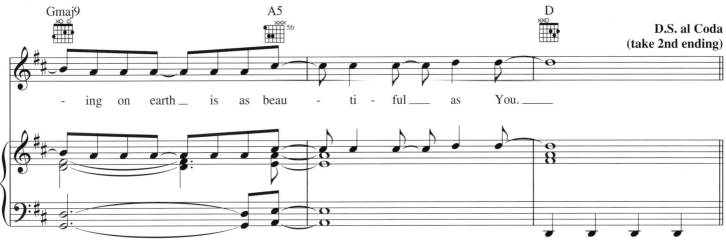

D.S. al Coda
(take 2nd ending)

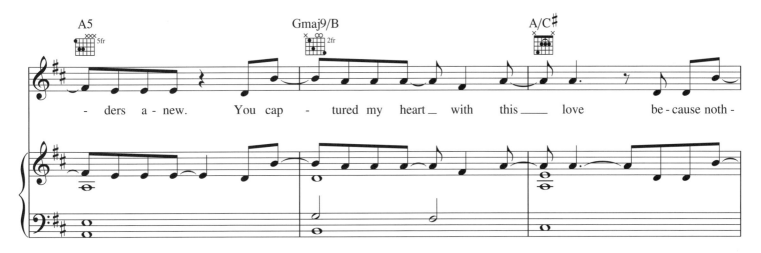

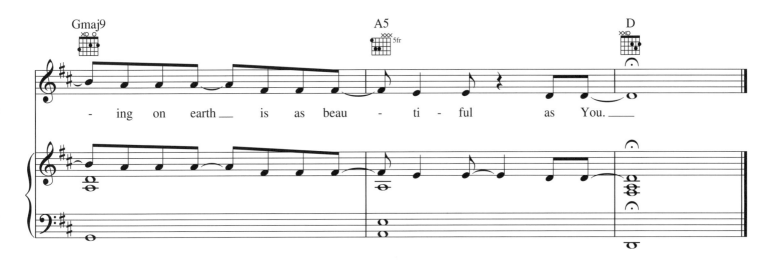

BLESSED BE YOUR NAME

Words and Music by MATT REDMAN
and BETH REDMAN

Steady four

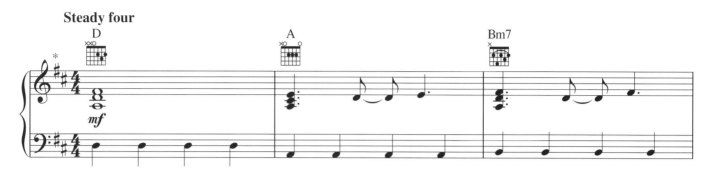

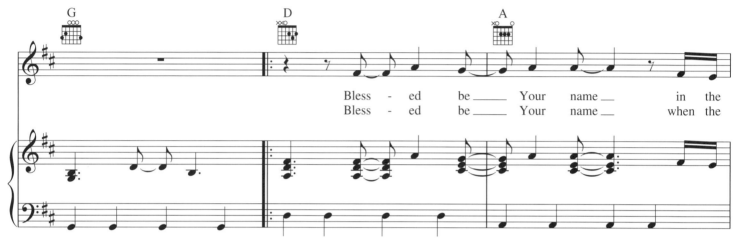

Bless - ed be _____ Your name _____ in the
Bless - ed be _____ Your name _____ when the

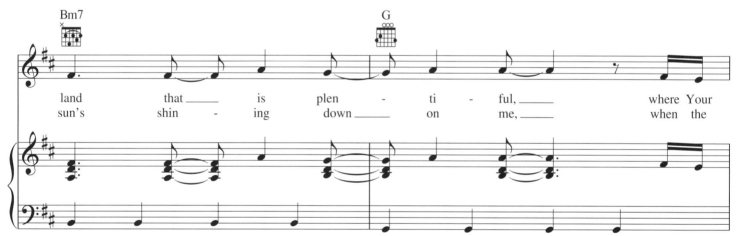

land that _____ is plen - ti - ful, _____ where Your
sun's shin - ing down _____ on me, _____ when the

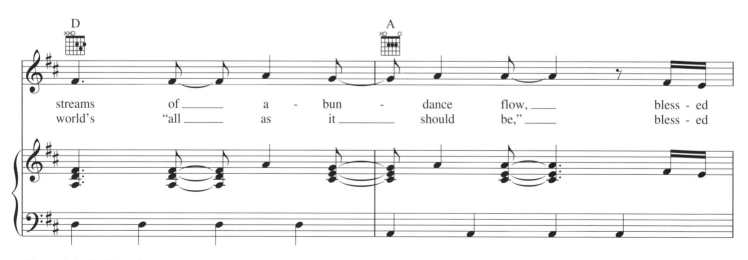

streams of _____ a - bun - dance flow, _____ bless - ed
world's "all _____ as it _____ should be," _____ bless - ed

Recorded a half step lower.

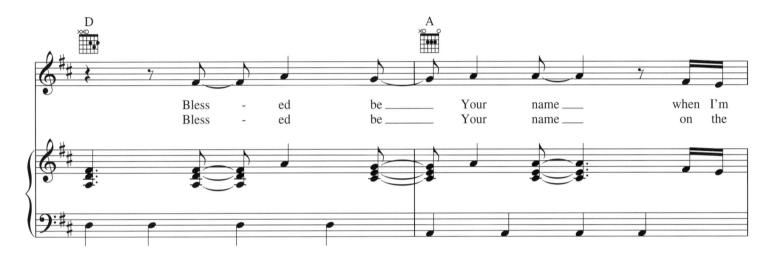

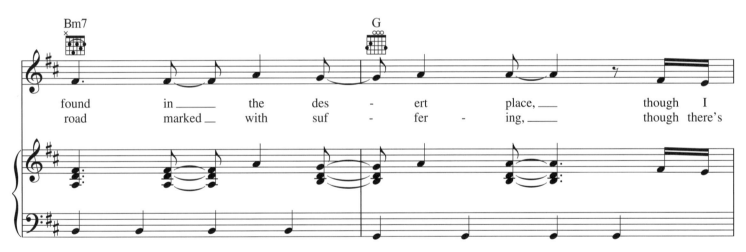

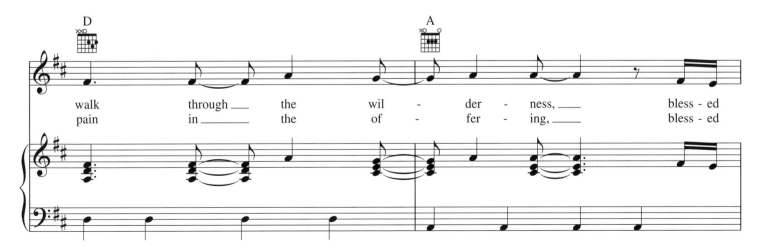

be Your name.
be Your name.

Ev - 'ry bless - ing

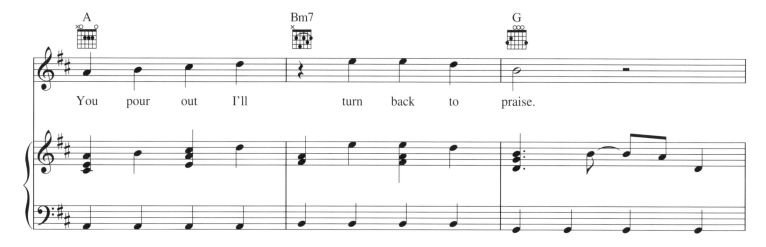

You pour out I'll turn back to praise.

When the dark - ness clos - es in, Lord, ___ still I will

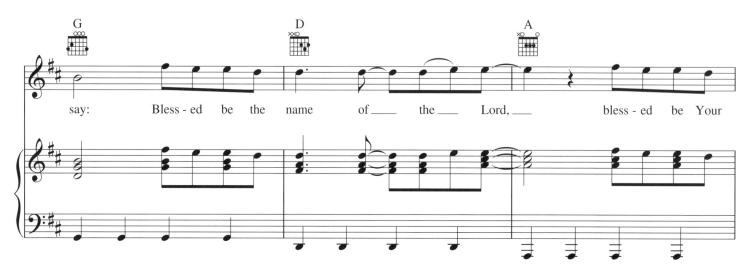

say: Bless - ed be the name of ___ the ___ Lord, ___ bless - ed be Your

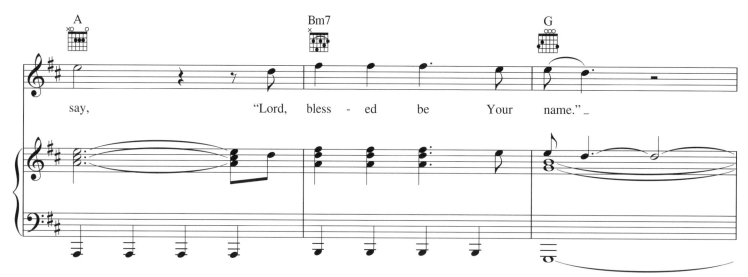

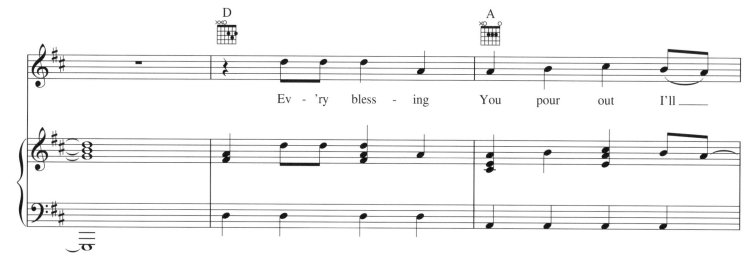

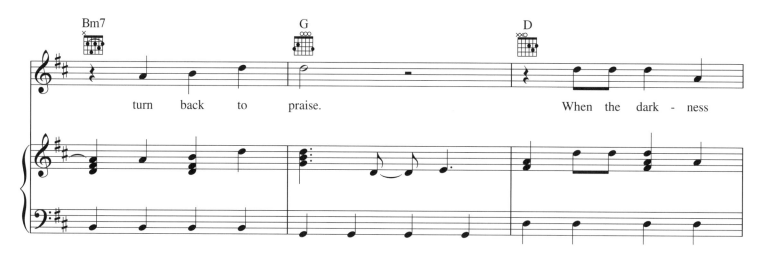

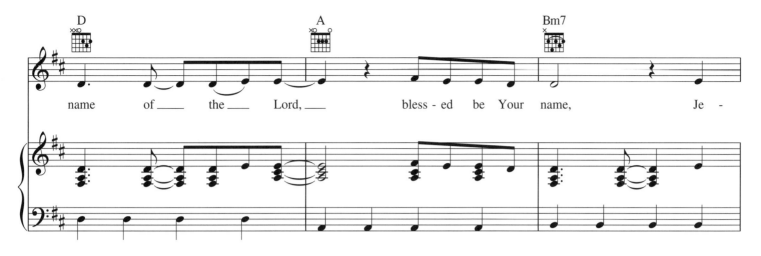

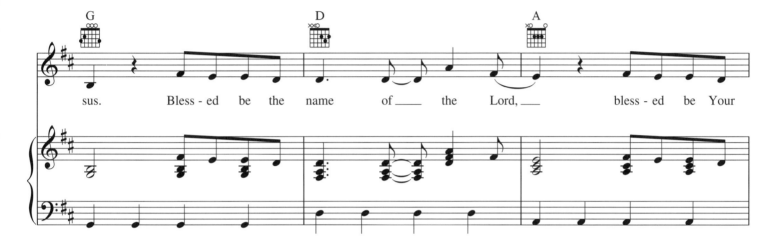

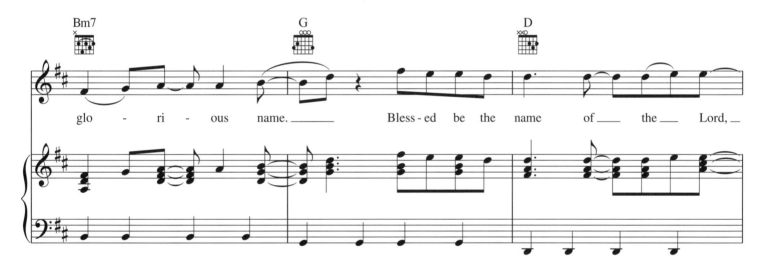

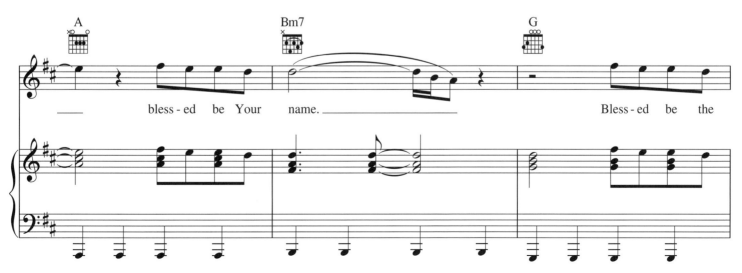

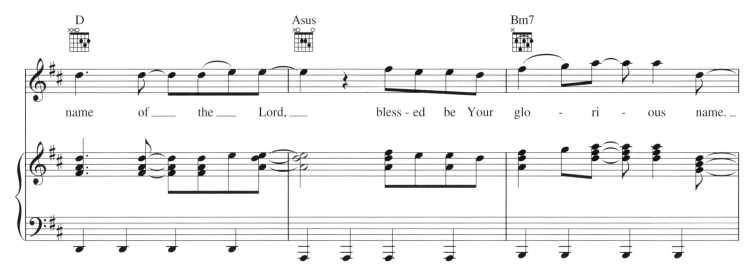

name of ___ the ___ Lord, ___ bless - ed be Your glo - ri - ous name. ___

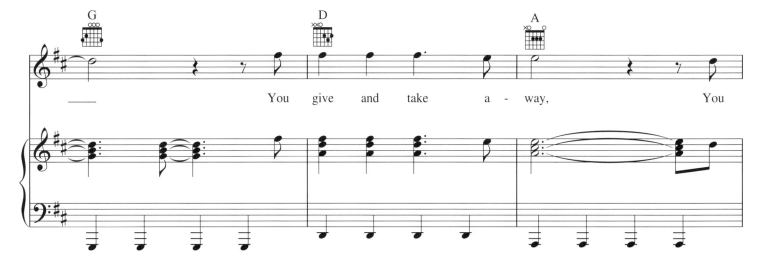

___ You give and take a - way, You

give and take a - way. ___ My heart will choose to

say, "Lord, bless - ed be Your name." _____ Yeah, yeah.

DRAW ME CLOSE

Words and Music by
KELLY CARPENTER

Warmly

With pedal

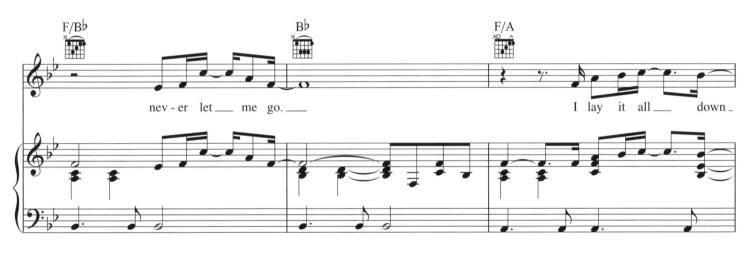

Draw me close __ to You, __ nev - er let __ me go. __ I lay it all __ down __

__ a - gain __ to hear You say __ that I'm __ Your friend. __

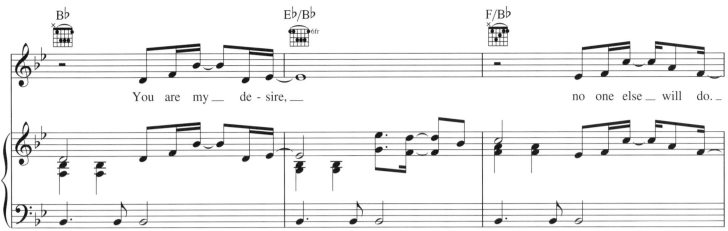

You are my __ de - sire, __ no one else __ will do. __

__ 'Cause noth - ing else __ could take __ Your place __

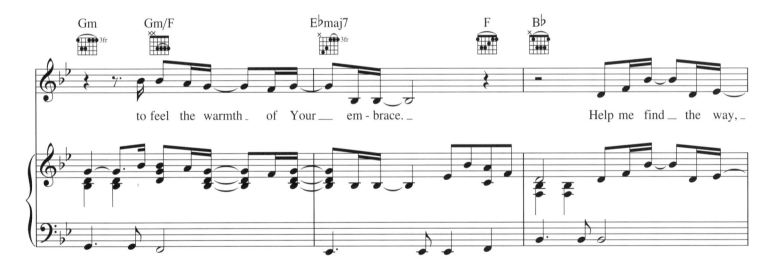

to feel the warmth __ of Your __ em - brace. __ Help me find __ the way, __

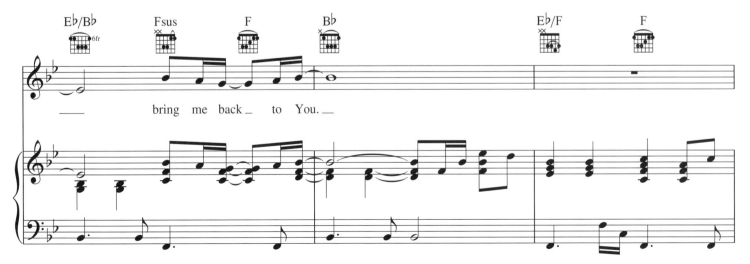

__ bring me back __ to You. __

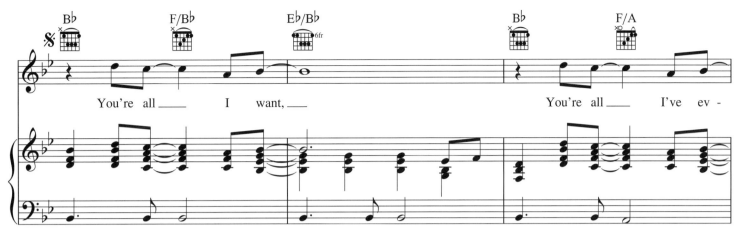

You're all ___ I want, ___ You're all ___ I've ev -

- er need - ed. You're all ___ I want. ___

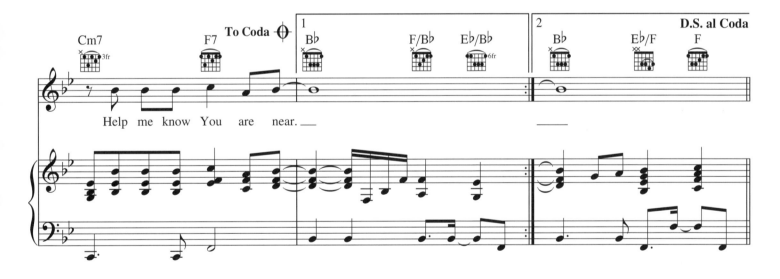

Help me know You are near. ___

Help me know You are near. ___

CLOSE TO YOUR HEART

Words and Music by
BEN CRIST

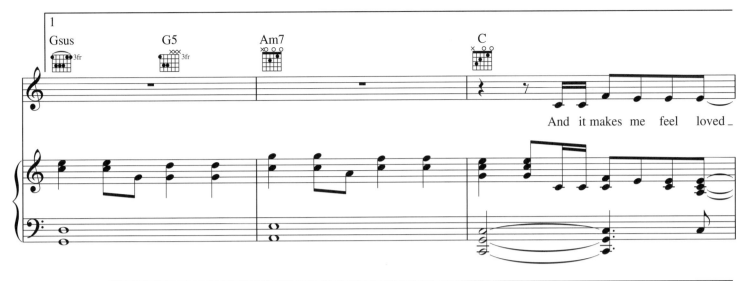

And it makes me feel loved

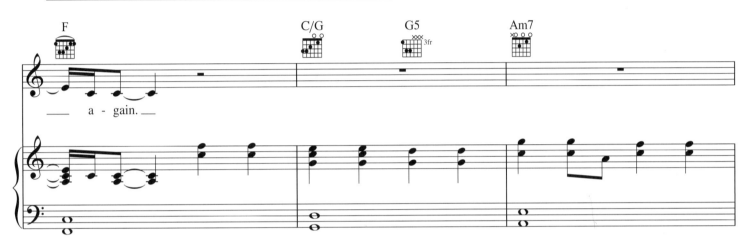

a - gain.

So close in Your arms.

And it makes me feel home a - gain,

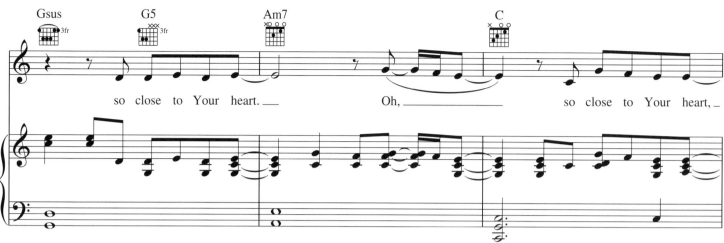

so close to Your heart. ___ Oh, _____ so close to Your heart, _

___ God.

So close to Your heart, ___ God. ___

So close to Your ___ heart, ___ I'm so close to Your ___ heart, _

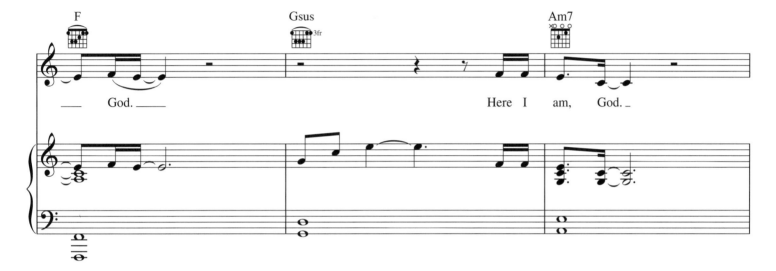

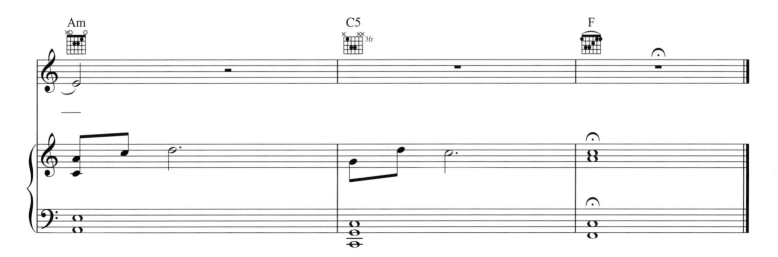

COME, NOW IS THE TIME TO WORSHIP

Words and Music by
BRIAN DOERKSEN

Moderate Rock

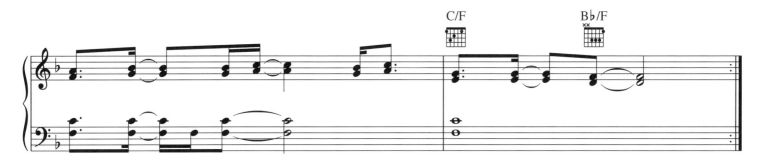

* *Recorded a half step lower.*

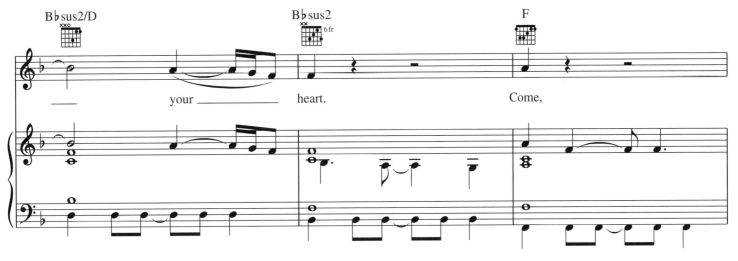

your _____ heart. Come,

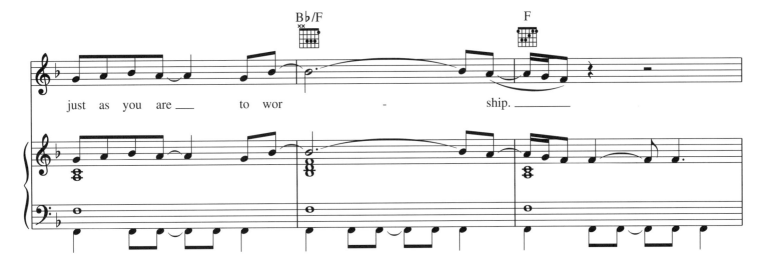

just as you are ___ to wor - ship. _____

Come, just as you are ___ be - fore ___ your _____

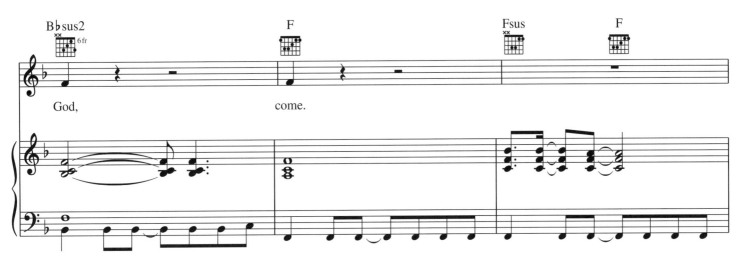

God, come.

One day eve-ry tongue will con-fess ___ You are God. ___

One day eve-ry knee ___ will bow. ___ Still the great-est treas-ure re-mains_

___ for those ___ who glad-ly choose_ You now. ___

___ glad-ly choose_ You now. ___

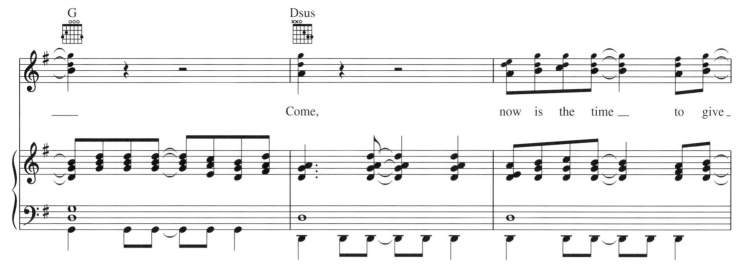

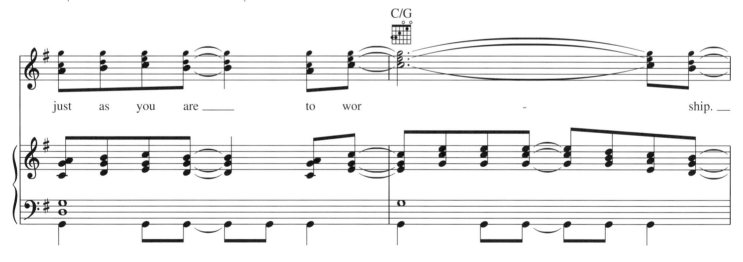

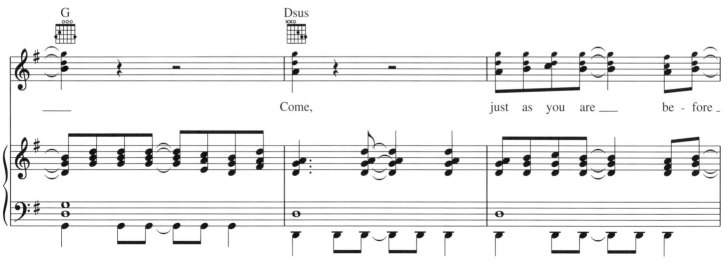

EVERLASTING GOD

Words and Music by BRENTON BROWN
and KEN RILEY

Recorded a half step lower.

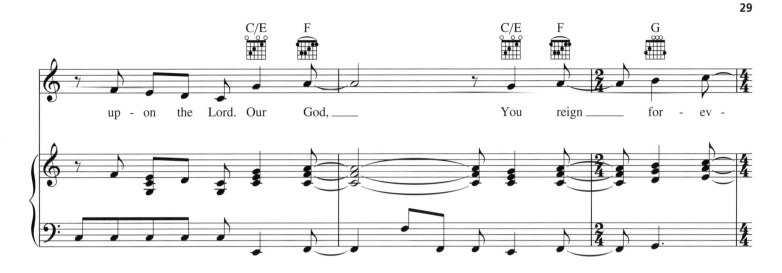

up - on the Lord. Our God, _____ You reign _____ for - ev -

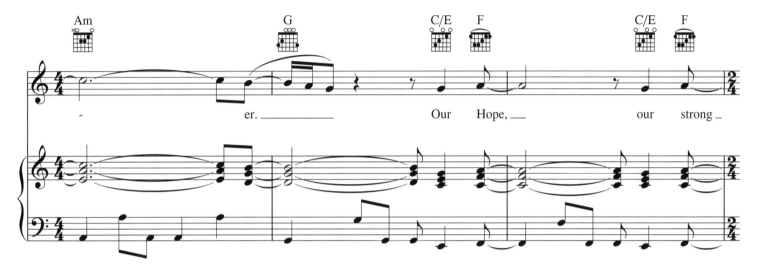

- er. _____ Our Hope, ___ our strong _

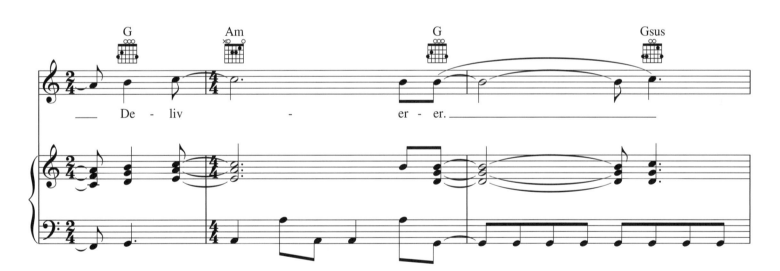

___ De - liv - er - er. _____

You are ___ the ev - er - last - ing God, ___ the ev -

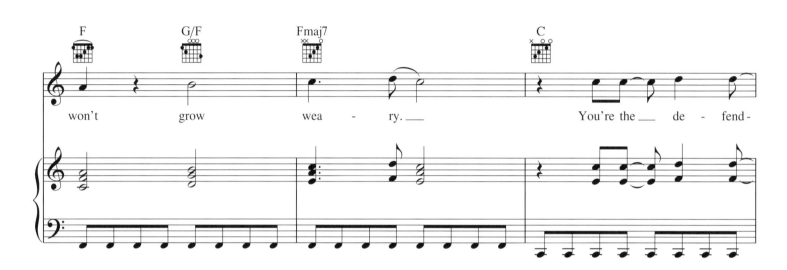

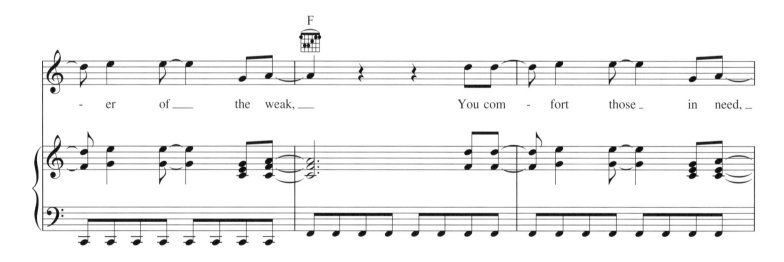

ea - gles. ____ ea - gles. ____

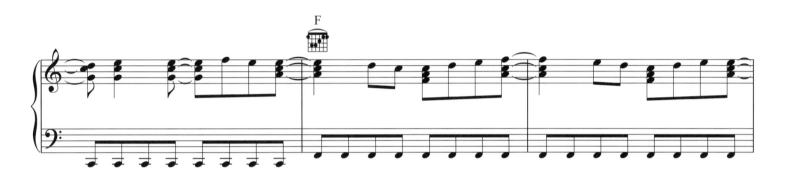

You are ____ the ev -

mp subito

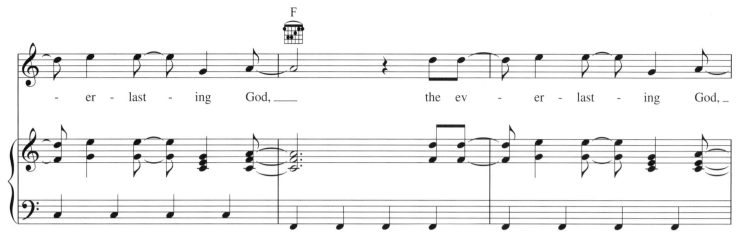

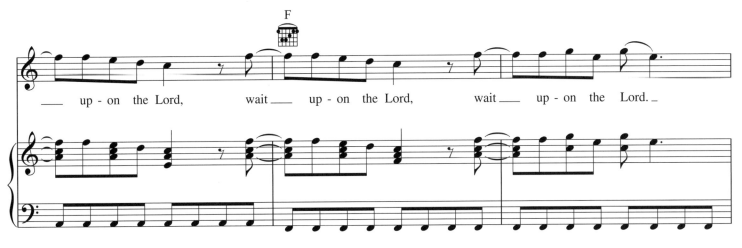

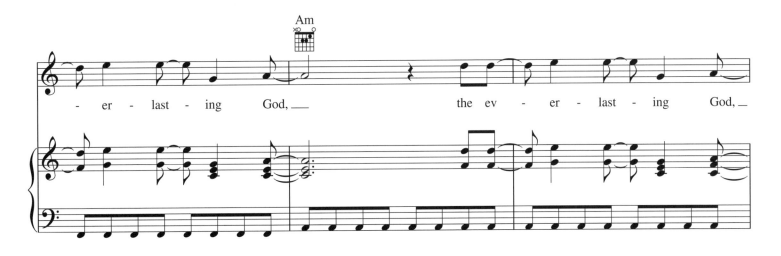

FOREVER

Words and Music by
CHRIS TOMLIN

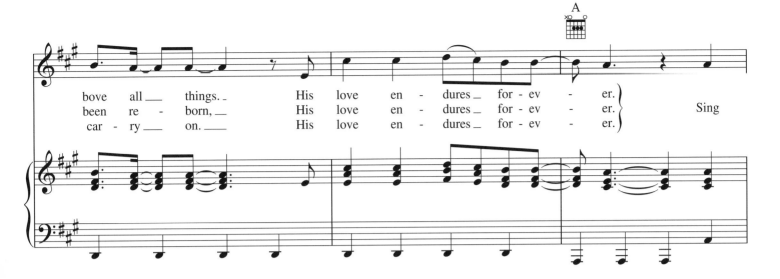

bove all __ things. __ His love en - dures __ for - ev - er.
been re - born, __ His love en - dures __ for - ev - er.
car - ry __ on. __ His love en - dures __ for - ev - er.
Sing

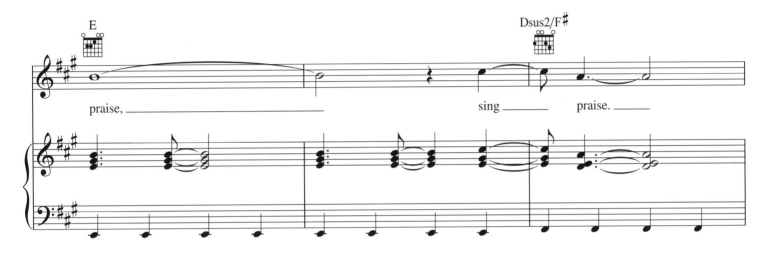

praise, _____ sing _____ praise. _____

Sing praise, _____

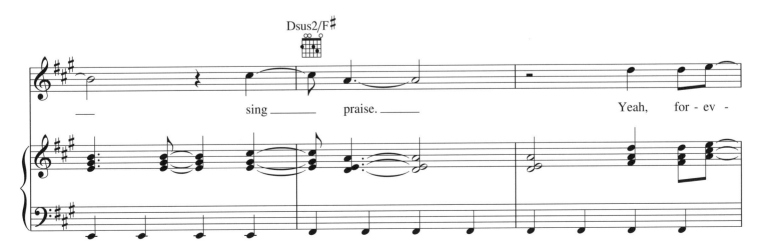

_____ sing _____ praise. _____ Yeah, for - ev -

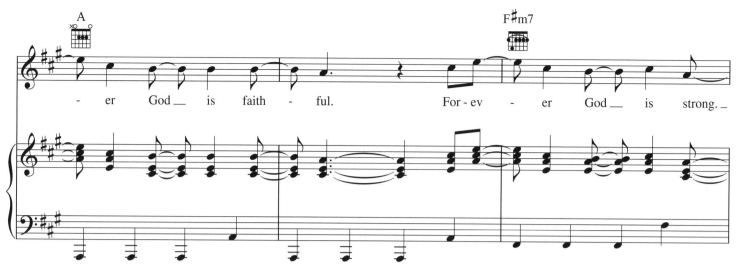

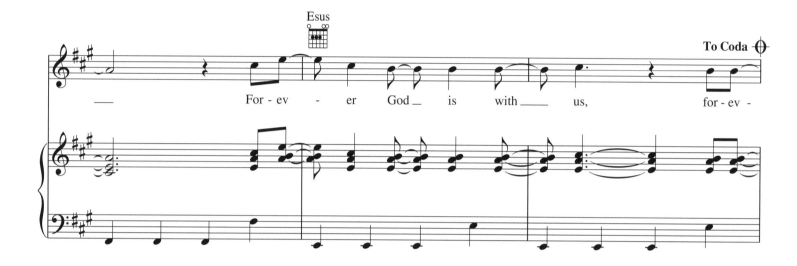

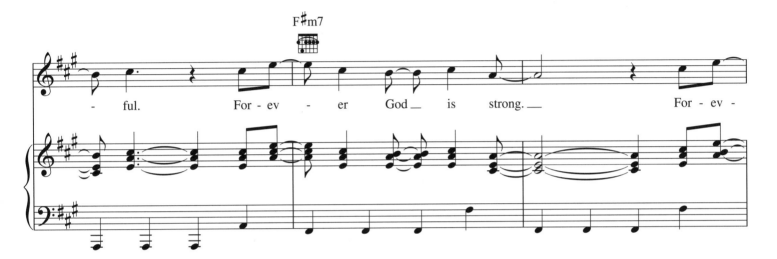

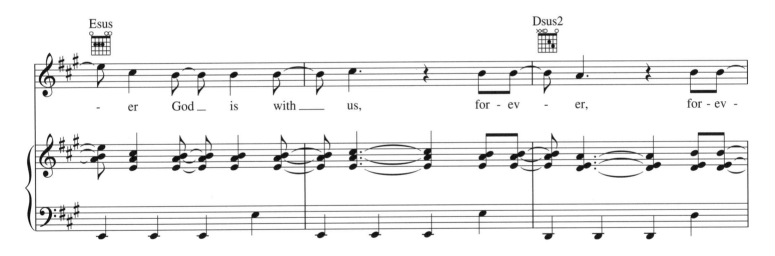

GOD OF WONDERS

Words and Music by MARC BYRD
and STEVE HINDALONG

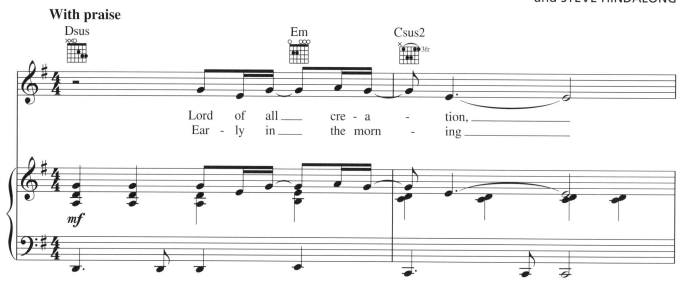

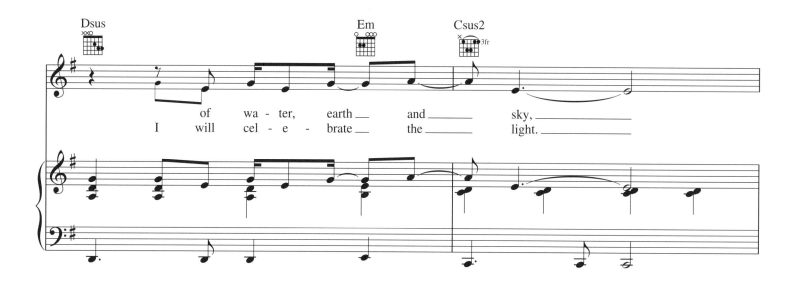

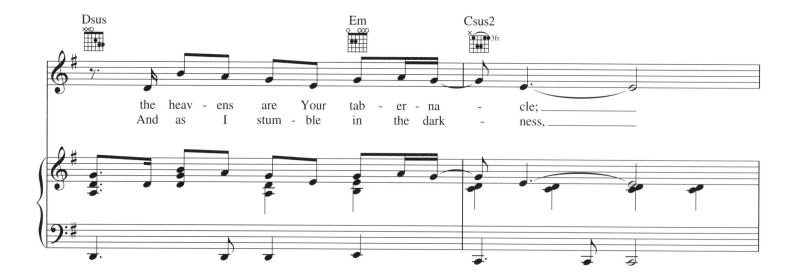

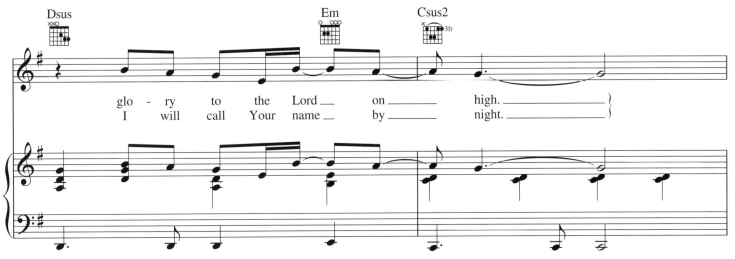

glo - ry to the Lord __ on __ high. __
I will call Your name __ by __ night. __

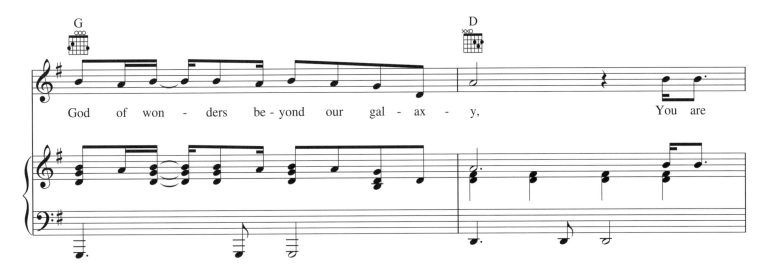

God of won - ders be - yond our gal - ax - y, You are

ho - ly, __ ho - ly. __ The

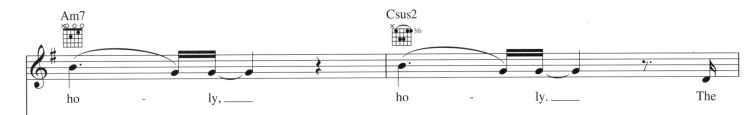

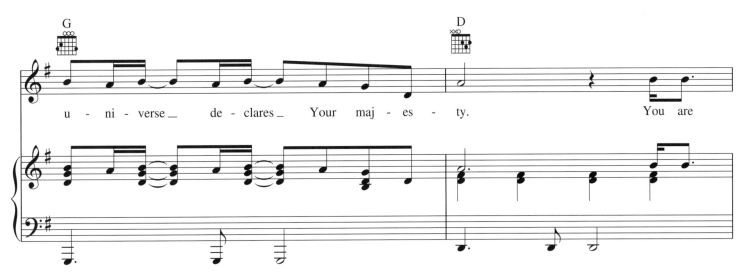

u - ni - verse __ de - clares __ Your maj - es - ty. You are

ho - ly, _____ ho - ly; _____

Lord of heav - en and _____ earth, _____

Lord of heav - en and _____ earth. _____

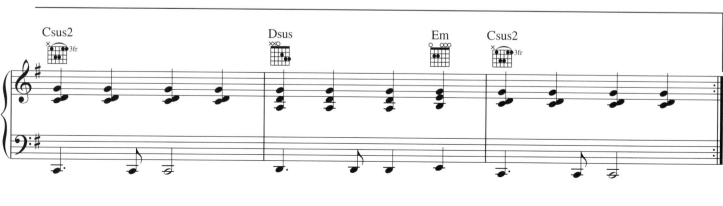

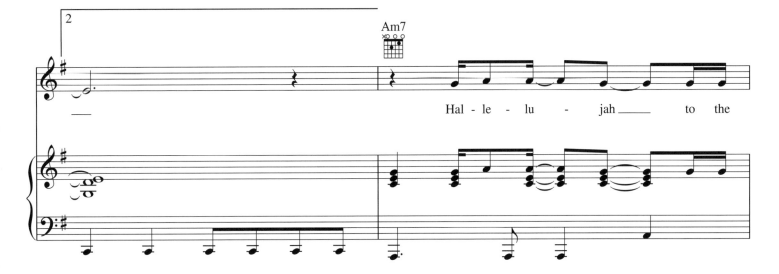

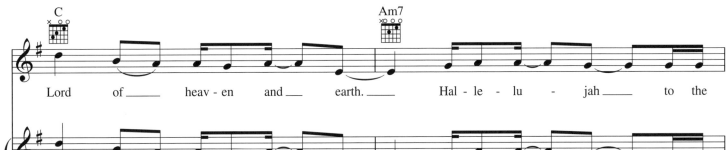

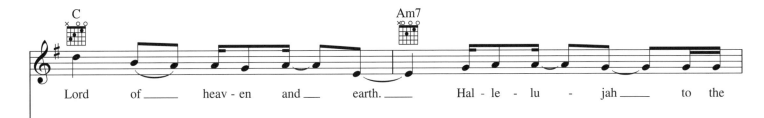

HAPPY DAY

Words and Music by TIM HUGHES
and BEN CANTELLON

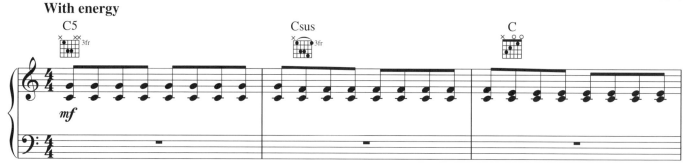

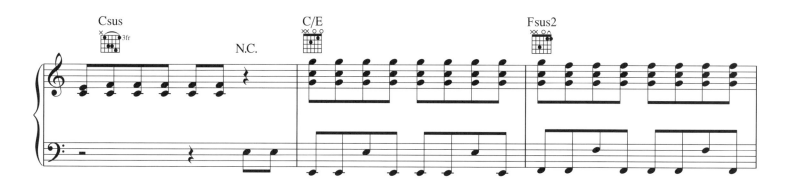

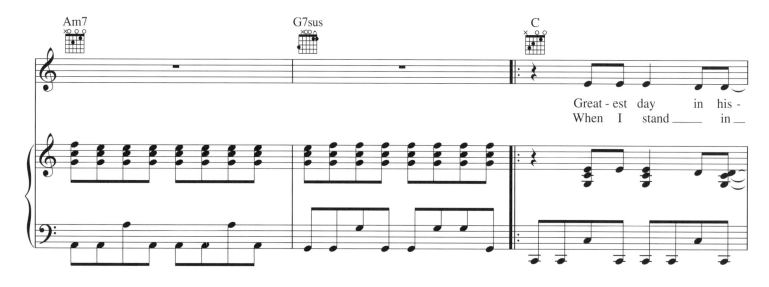

Great- est day in his-
When I stand ____ in ____

- to - ry;   death is beat- en,   You ____ have res- cued   me. ____
____ that place,   free at last, ____ meet- ing face ___ to   face, ____

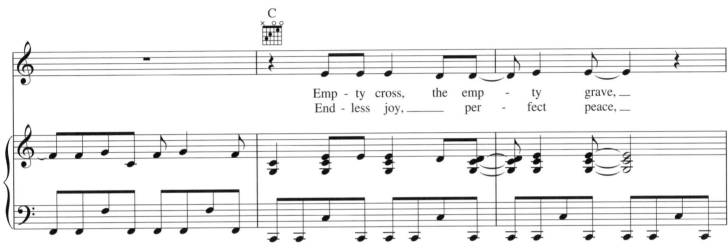

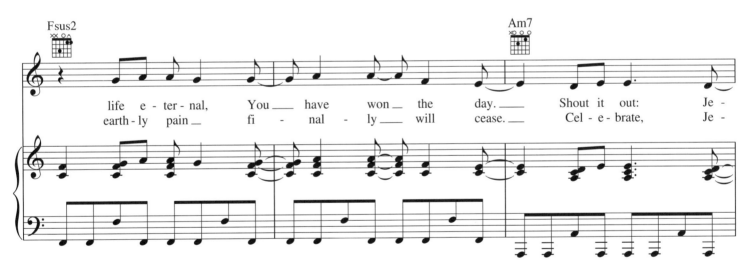

44

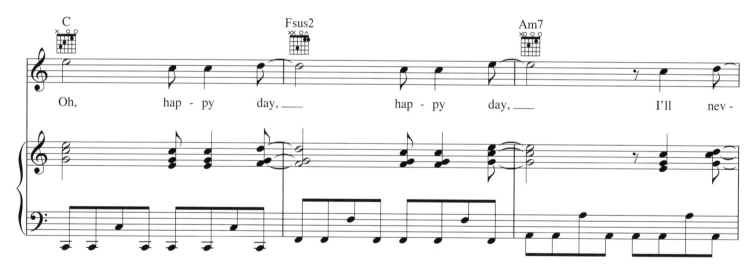

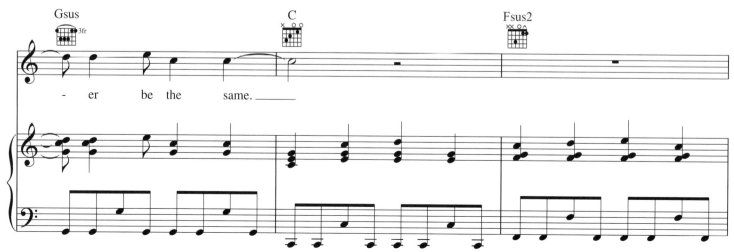

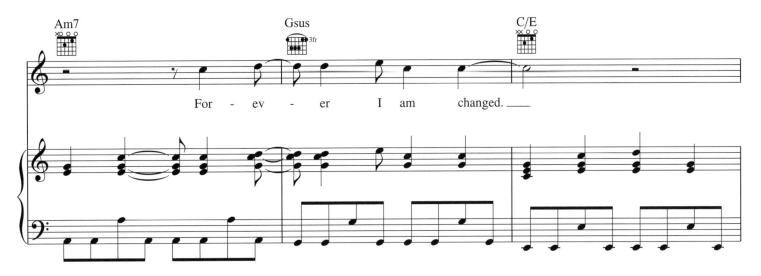

For - ev - er I am changed. ____

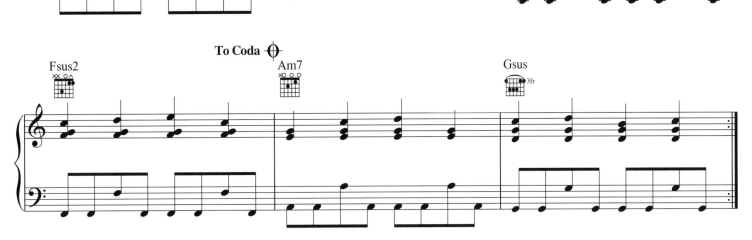

To Coda ⊕

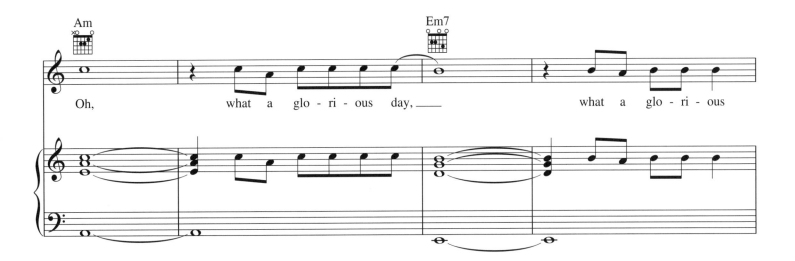

Oh, what a glo - ri - ous day, ____ what a glo - ri - ous

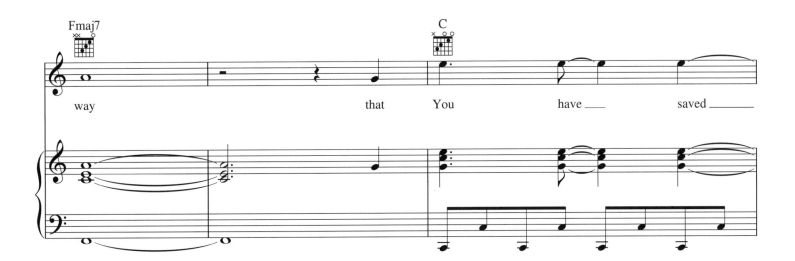

way that You have ____ saved ____

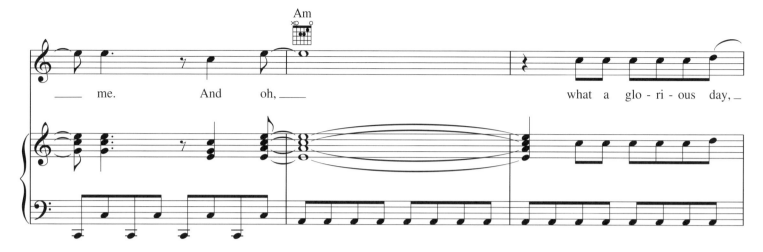

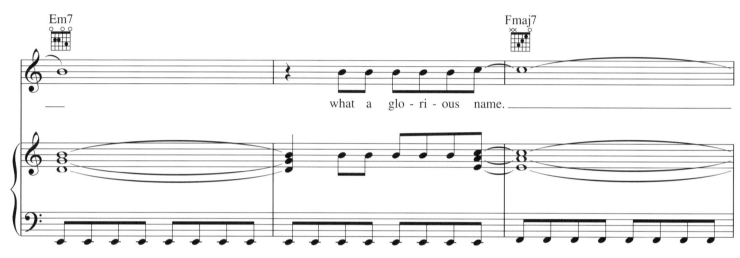

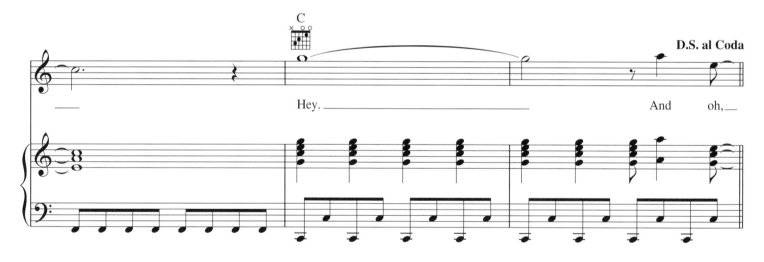

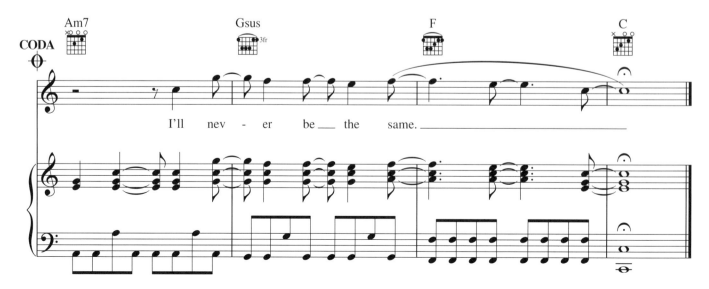

HE REIGNS

Words and Music by PETER FURLER
and STEVE TAYLOR

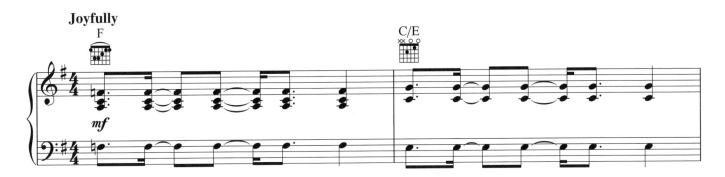

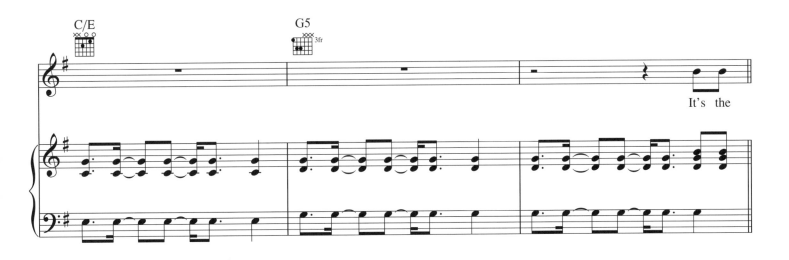

It's the

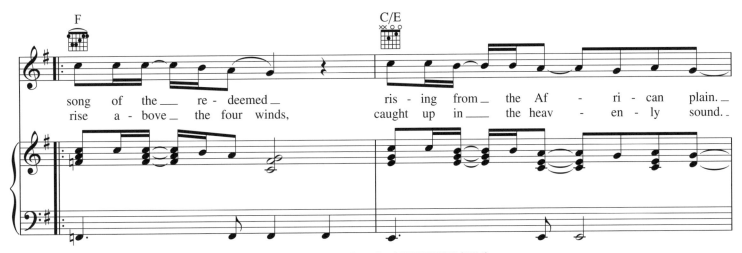

song of the __ re - deemed __ rising from __ the Af - ri - can plain. __
rise a - bove __ the four winds, caught up in __ the heav - en - ly sound. __

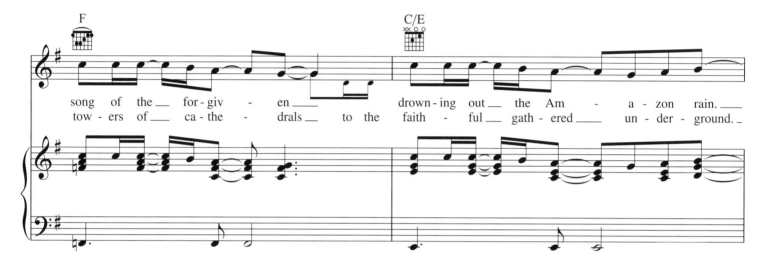

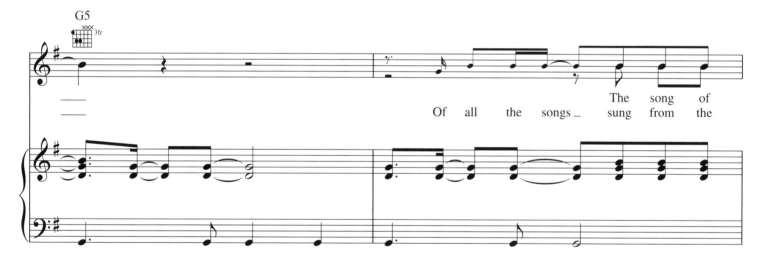

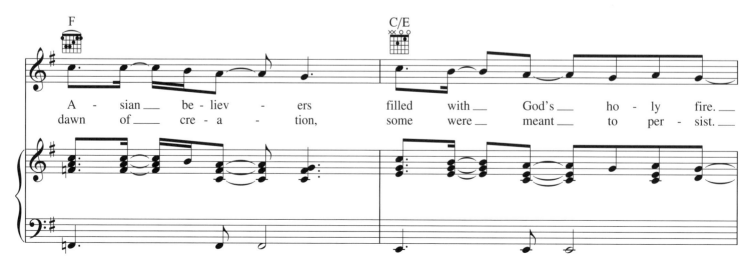

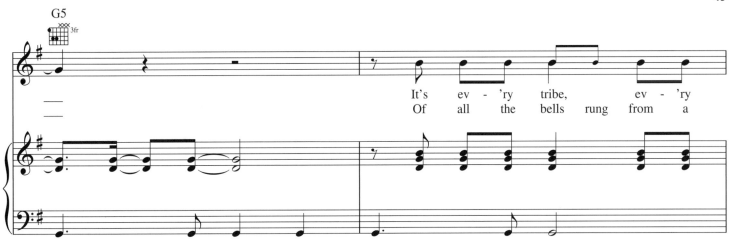

It's ev-'ry tribe, ev-'ry
Of all the bells rung from a

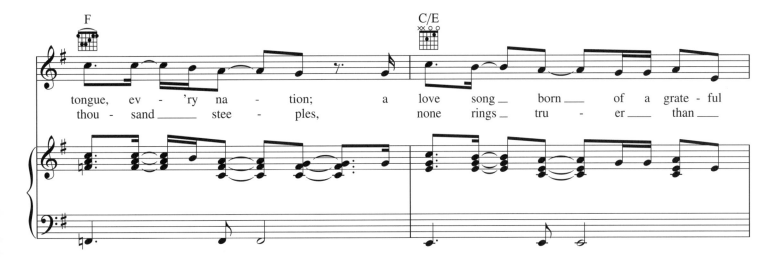

tongue, ev-'ry na - tion; a love song __ born __ of a grate-ful
thou - sand __ stee - ples, none rings __ tru - er __ than __

choir.
this.
It's all God's chil-dren sing-ing, "Glo - ry, glo - ry,

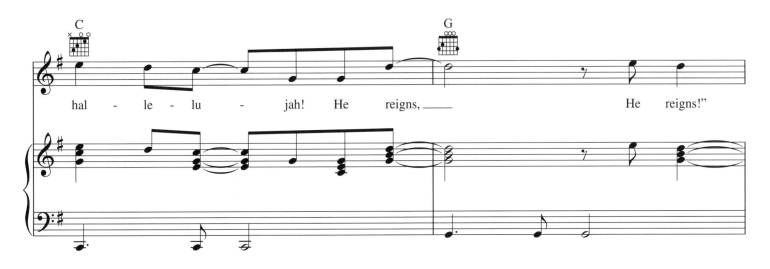

hal - le - lu - jah! He reigns, ___ He reigns!"

It's all God's chil - dren sing - ing, "Glo - ry, glo - ry,

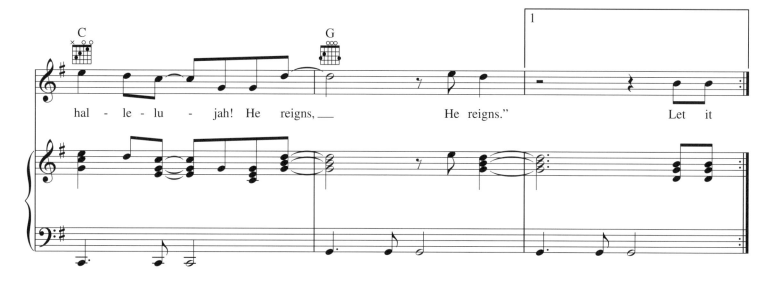

hal - le - lu - jah! He reigns, ___ He reigns." Let it

It's all God's chil - dren sing - ing, "Glo - ry, glo - ry,

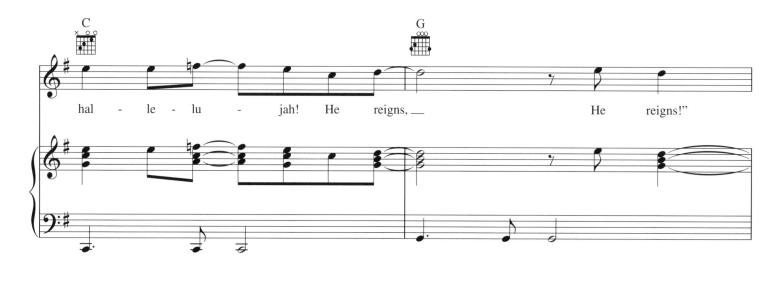

hal - le - lu - jah! He reigns, ___ He reigns!"

It's all God's chil-dren sing-ing, "Glo - ry, glo - ry,

hal - le - lu - jah! He reigns, ____ He reigns." And all the

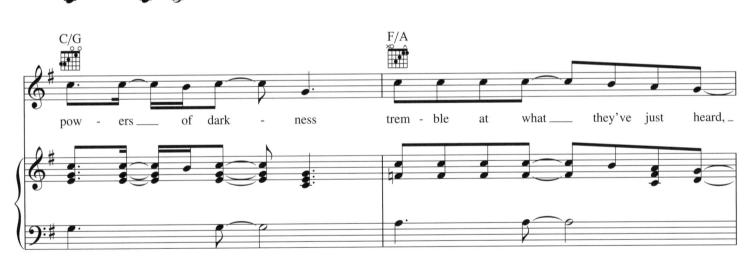

pow - ers ___ of dark - ness trem - ble at what ___ they've just heard, ___

___ 'cause all the

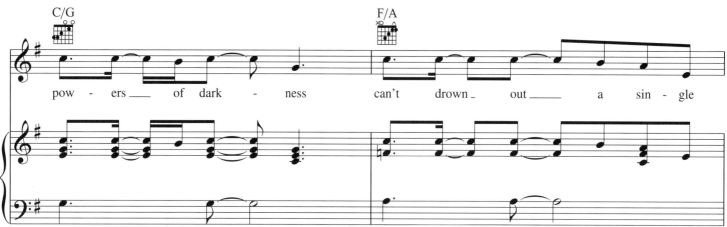

pow - ers ___ of dark - ness can't drown __ out ___ a sin - gle

word. ___ When all God's chil - dren sing out,

"Glo - ry, glo - ry, hal - le - lu - jah! He reigns, ___ He reigns!"

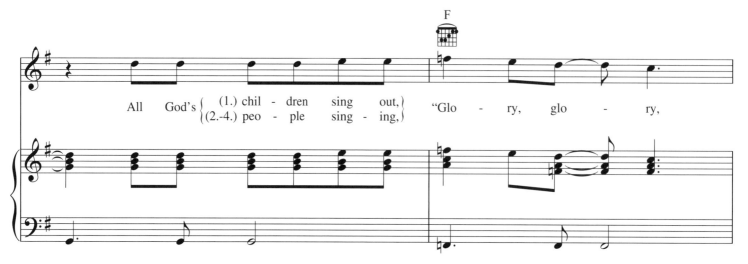

All God's { (1.) chil - dren sing out,} "Glo - ry, glo - ry,
{ (2.-4.) peo - ple sing - ing,}

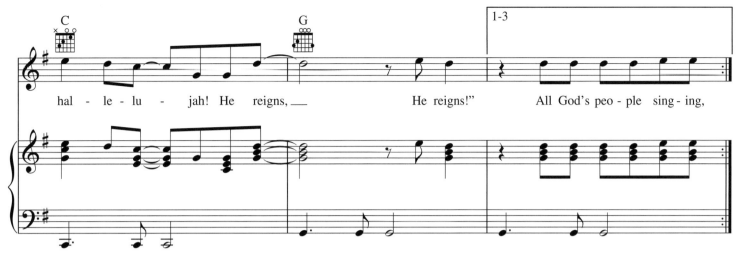

hal - le - lu - jah! He reigns, ___ He reigns!" All God's peo - ple sing - ing,

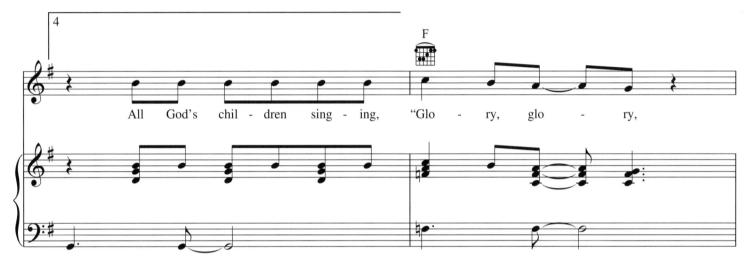

All God's chil - dren sing - ing, "Glo - ry, glo - ry,

hal - le - lu - jah! He reigns, ___ He reigns!" All God's chil - dren sing - ing,

"Glo - ry, glo - ry, hal - le - lu - jah! He reigns!" ___

HE IS EXALTED

Words and Music by
TWILA PARIS

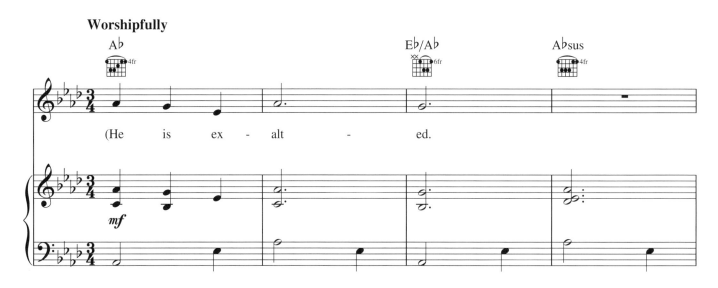

(He is ex - alt - ed.

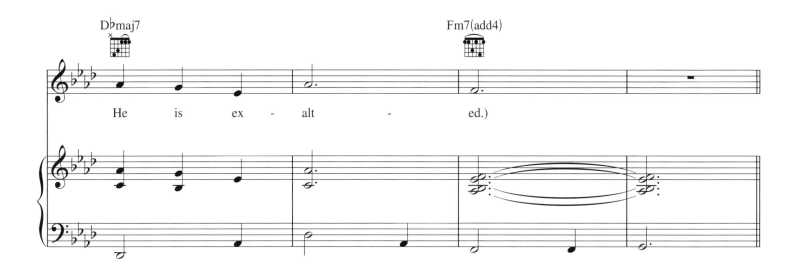

He is ex - alt - ed.)

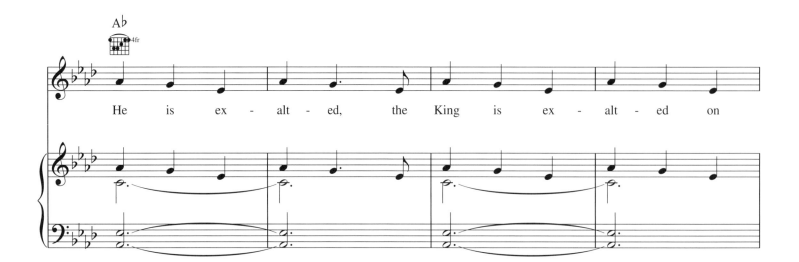

He is ex - alt - ed, the King is ex - alt - ed on

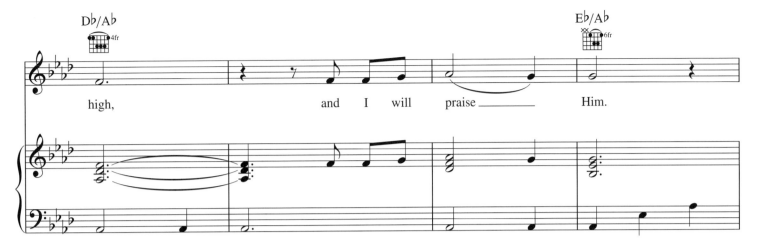

high, and I will praise _____ Him.

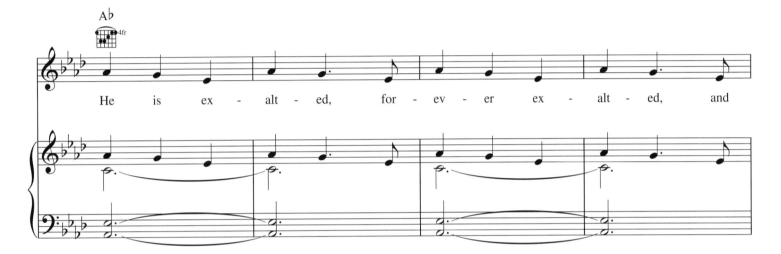

He is ex - alt - ed, for - ev - er ex - alt - ed, and

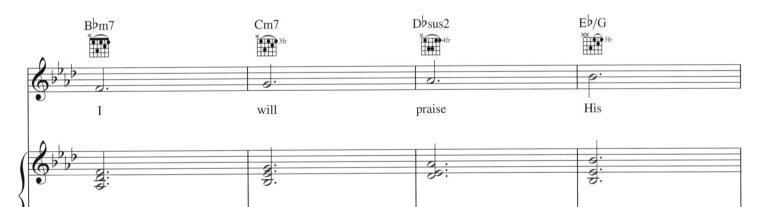

I will praise His

name! _____ For

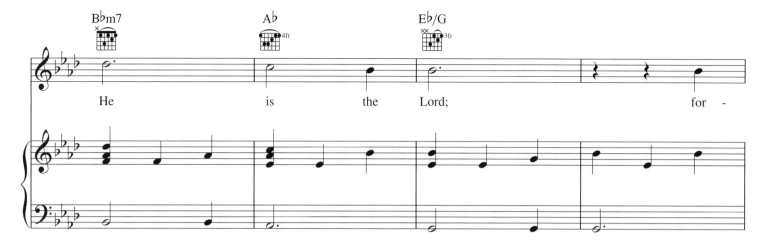

He is the Lord; for -

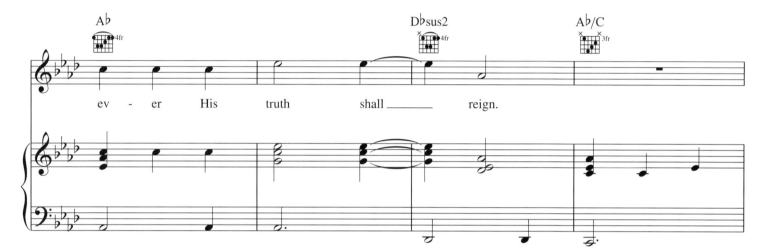

ev - er His truth shall _____ reign.

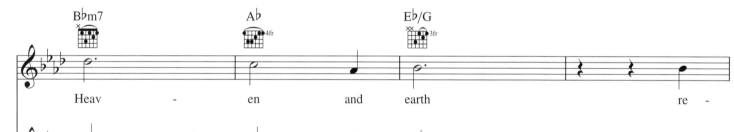

Heav - en and earth re -

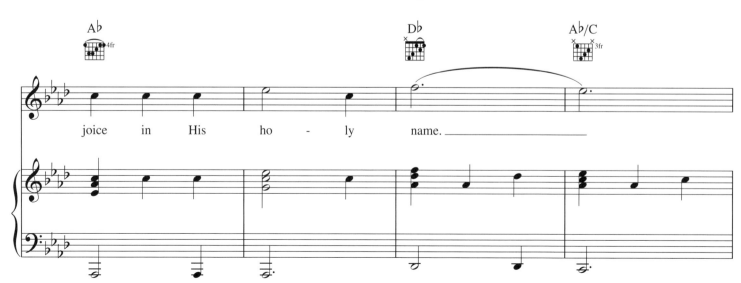

joice in His ho - ly name. _____

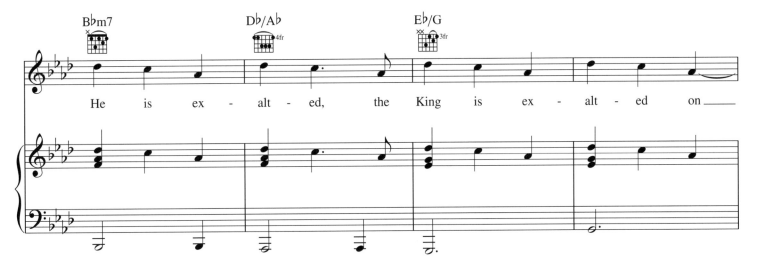

He is ex - alt - ed, the King is ex - alt - ed on

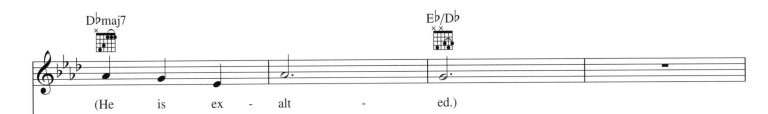

high.

(He is ex - alt - ed.)

He is ex - alt - ed, the King is ex - alt - ed on

high, and I will praise Him.

He is ex - alt - ed, for - ev - er ex - alt - ed, and

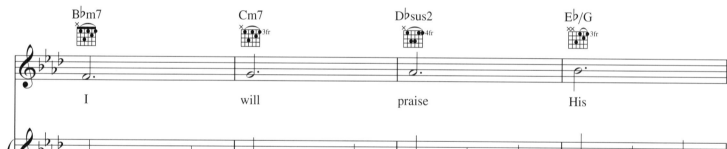

I will praise His

name! For

He is ex - alt - ed. the

King is ex - alt - ed on high.

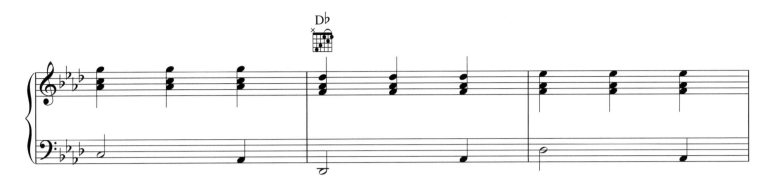

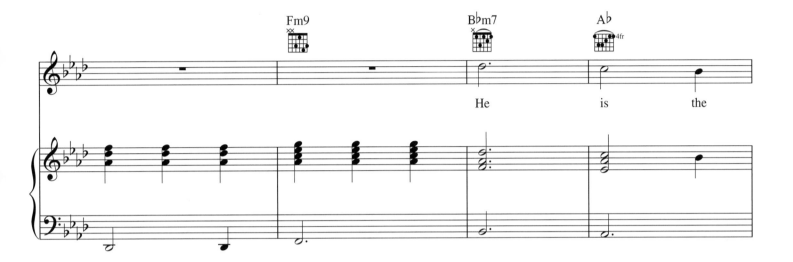

He is the

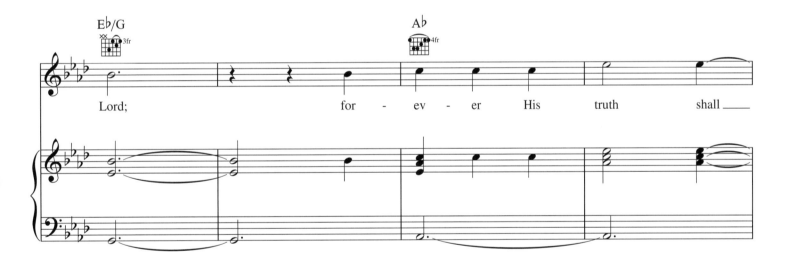

Lord; for - ev - er His truth shall _____

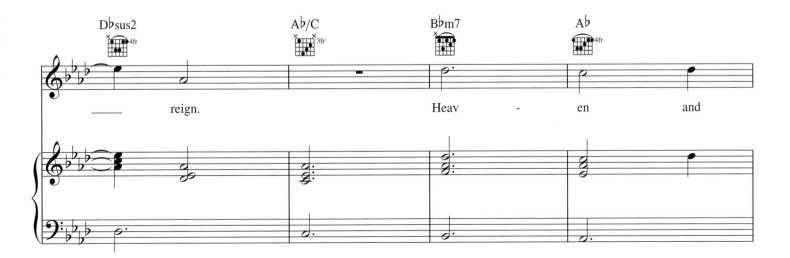

_____ reign. Heav - en and

62

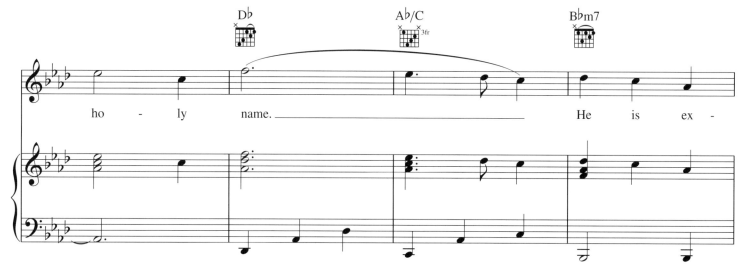

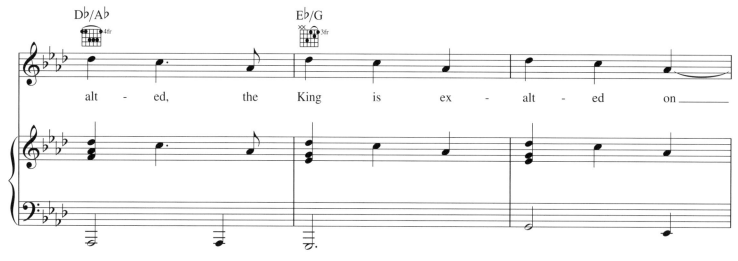

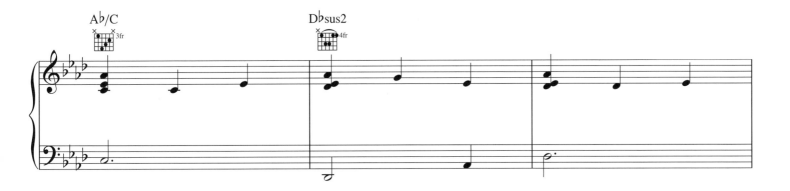

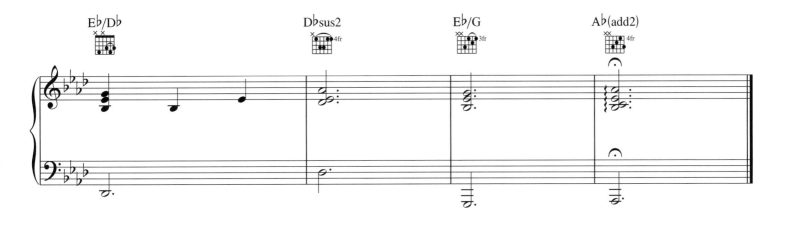

HOLY IS THE LORD

Words and Music by CHRIS TOMLIN
and LOUIE GIGLIO

With praise

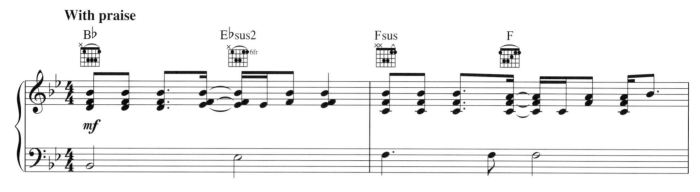

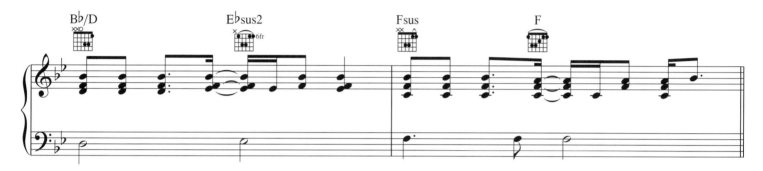

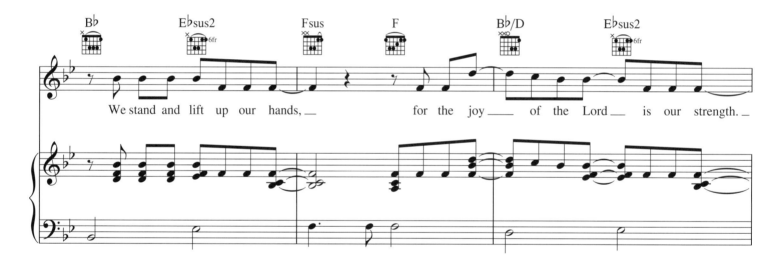

We stand and lift up our hands, ___ for the joy ___ of the Lord ___ is our strength. ___

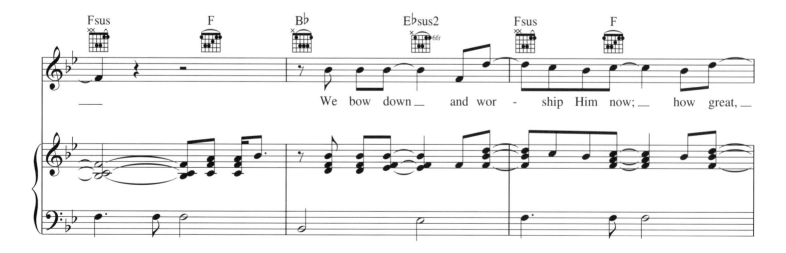

___ We bow down ___ and wor - ship Him now; ___ how great, ___

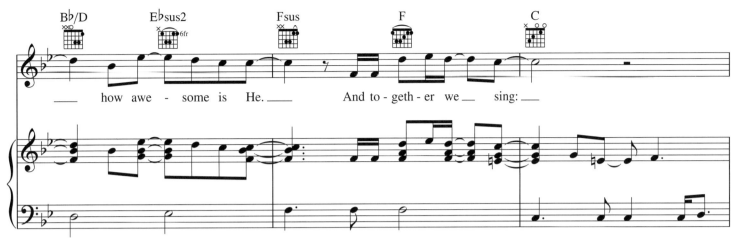

how aw - e - some is He. ___ And to - geth - er we ___ sing: ___

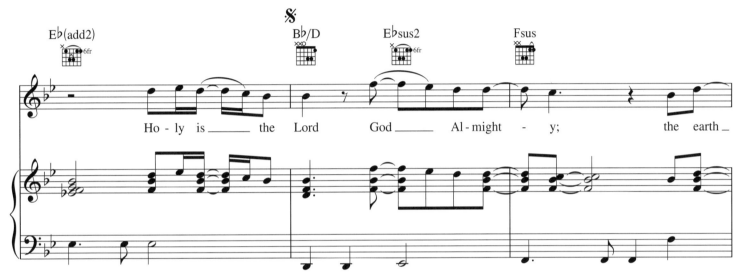

Ho - ly is ___ the Lord God ___ Al - might - y; ___ the earth ___

___ is filled ___ with His glo - ry. Ho - ly is ___ the Lord God ___ Al - might -

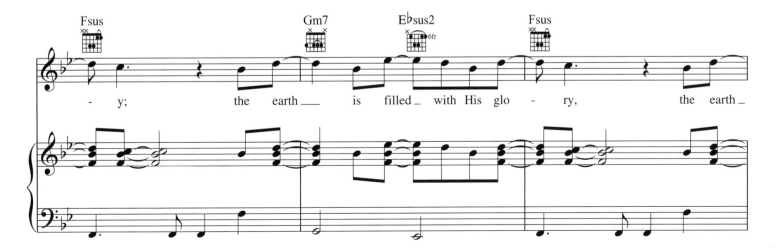

- y; ___ the earth ___ is filled ___ with His glo - ry, ___ the earth ___

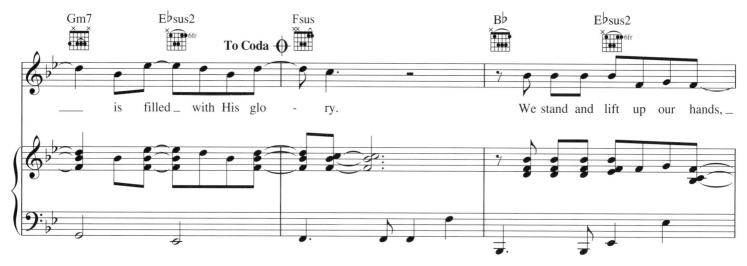

is filled _ with His glo - ry. We stand and lift up our hands, _

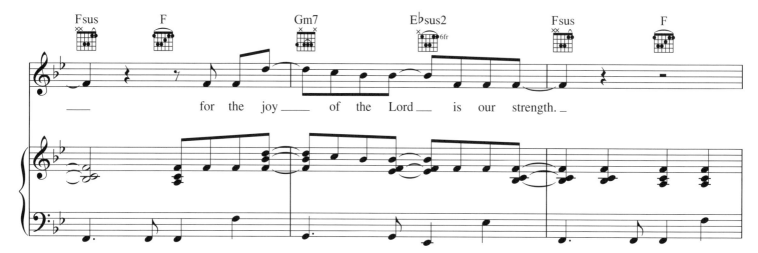

_ for the joy _ of the Lord _ is our strength. _

We bow down _ and wor - ship Him now; _ how great, _ how awe - some is He. _

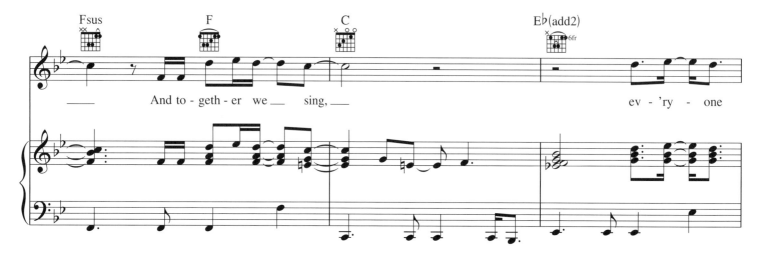

_ And to - geth - er we _ sing, _ ev - 'ry - one

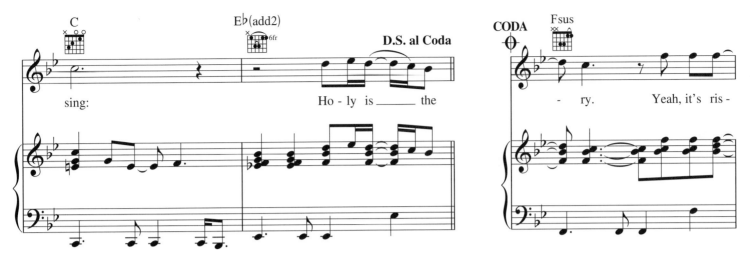

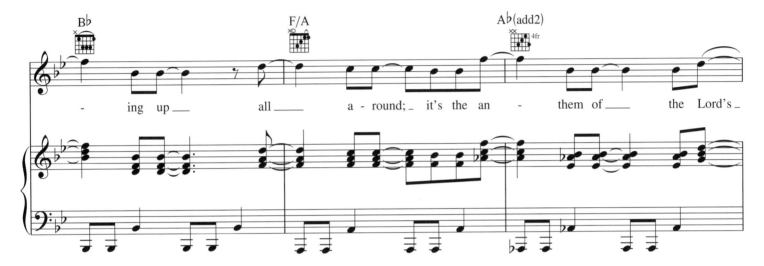

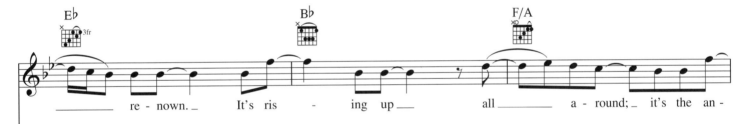

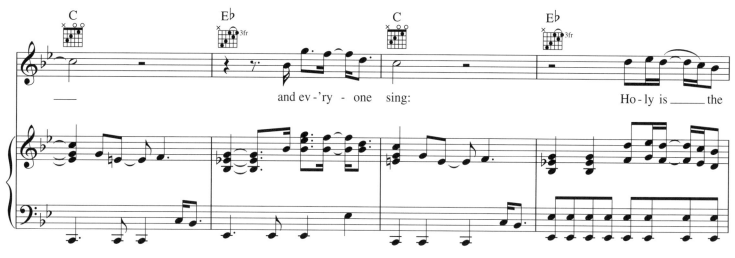

and ev-'ry - one sing: Ho - ly is _____ the

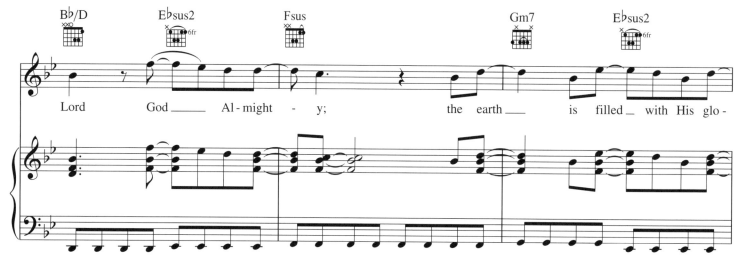

Lord God _____ Al - might - y; the earth _____ is filled _ with His glo-

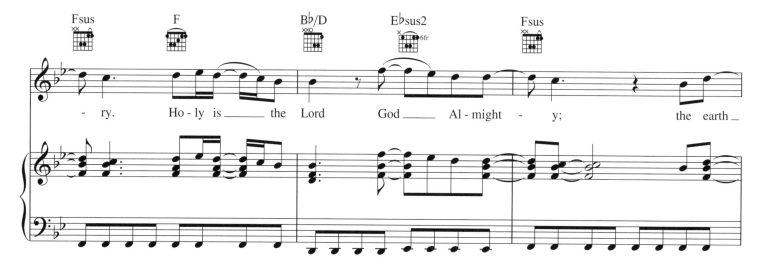

- ry. Ho - ly is _____ the Lord God _____ Al - might - y; the earth _

_____ is filled _ with His glo - ry, the earth _____ is filled _ with His glo-

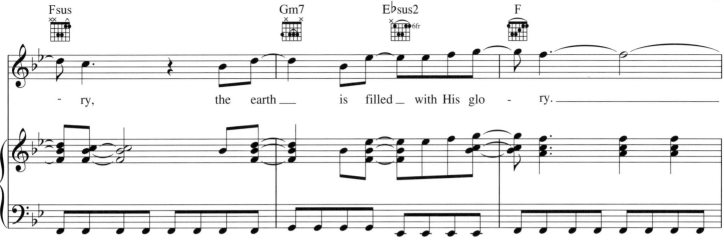

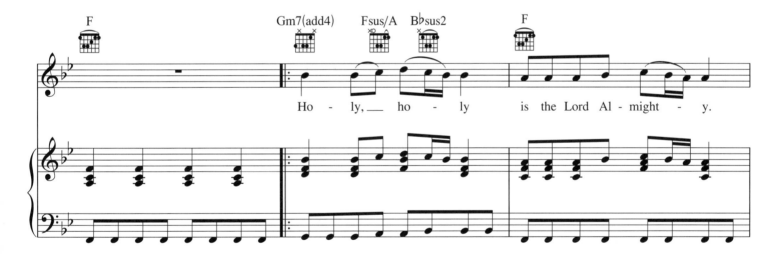

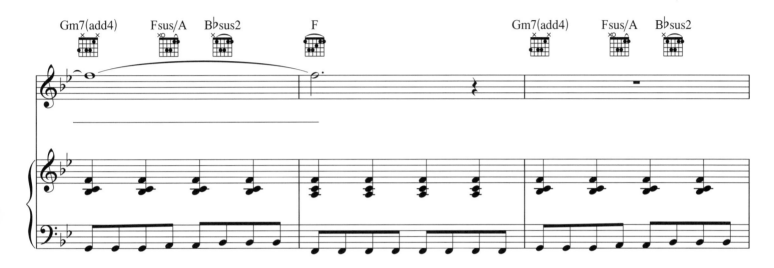

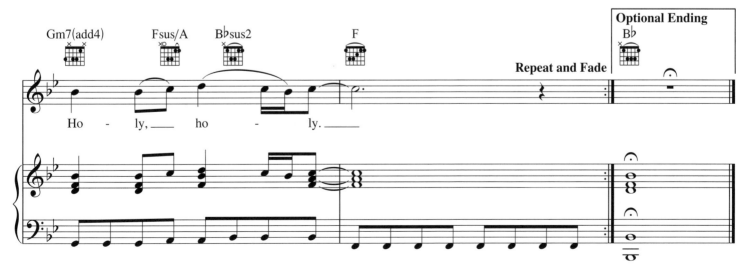

HOSANNA

Words and Music by
BROOKE FRASER

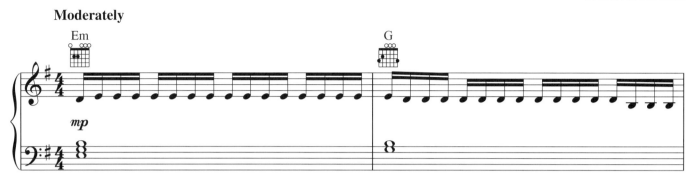

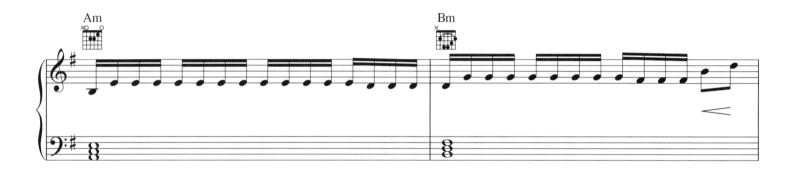

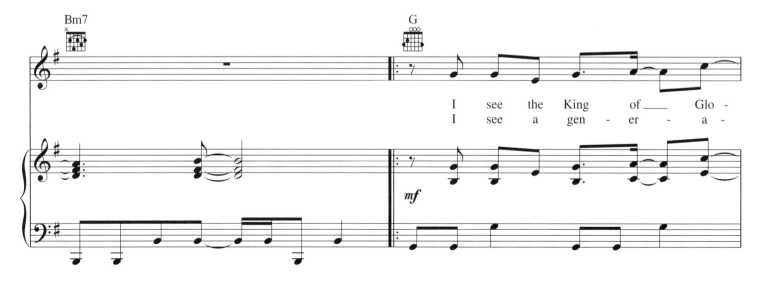

I see the King of ___ Glo-
I see a gen- er- a-

Em

-ry | com - ing on the clouds with ___ fire; ___
-tion | ris - ing up to take their ___ place ___

Am7

the whole earth shakes, ___ the whole earth shakes. ___
with self - less faith, ___ self - less faith. ___

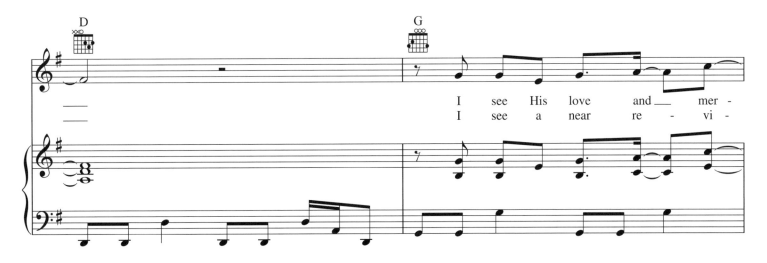

D   G

I see His love and ___ mer -
I see a near re - vi -

Em

-cy ___ wash - ing o - ver all our ___ sin; ___
-val ___ stir - ring as we pray and ___ sing; ___

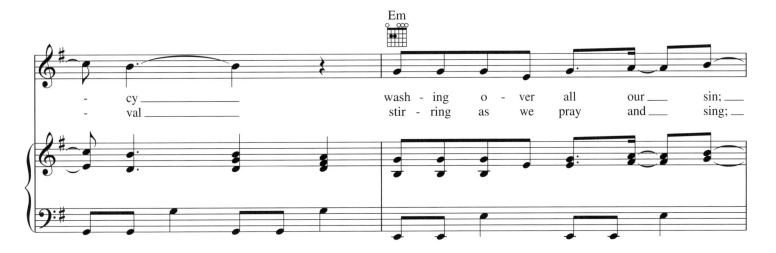

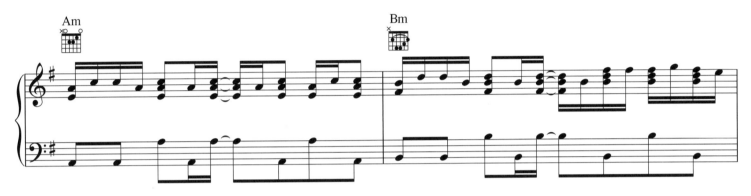

Heal my heart and make it _____ clean, _____

o - pen up my eyes to the things un - seen. ____

Show me how to love like __ You __ have loved __ me. __

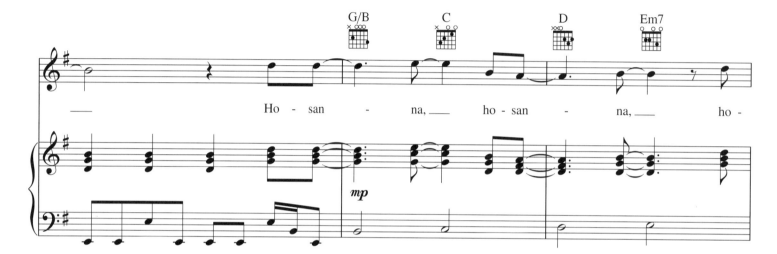

__ Ho - san - na, __ ho - san - na, __ ho -

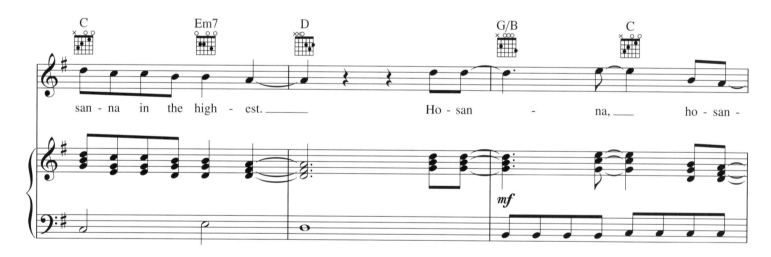

san - na in the high - est. __ Ho - san - na, __ ho - san -

D.S. al Coda

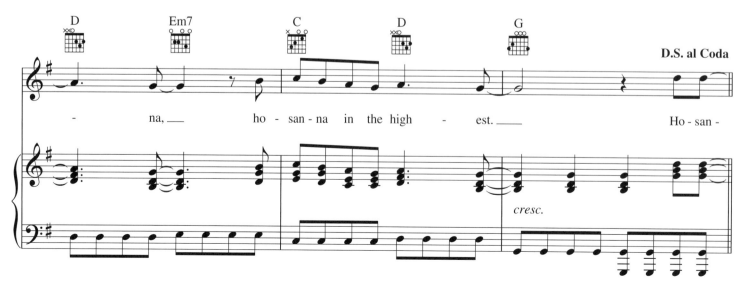

- na, __ ho - san - na in the high - est. __ Ho - san -

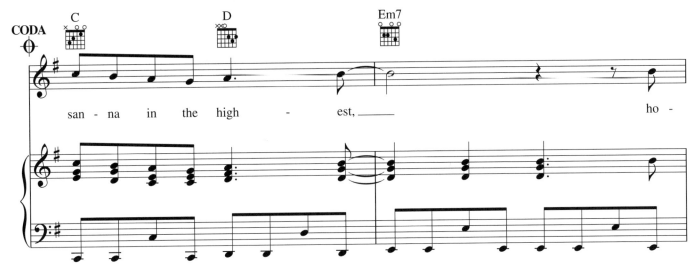

san - na in the high - est, _____ ho -

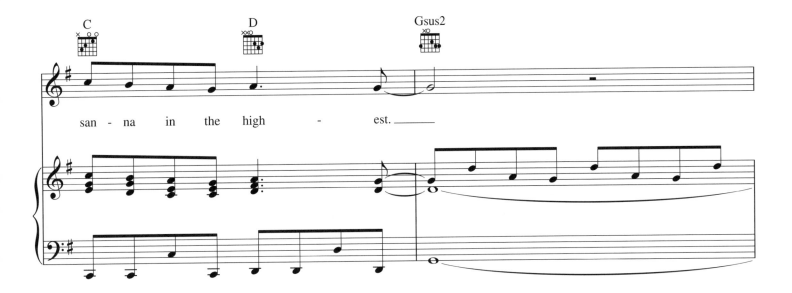

san - na in the high - est. _____

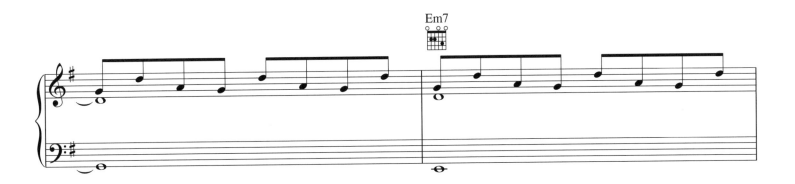

HOW DEEP THE FATHER'S LOVE FOR US

Words and Music by
STUART TOWNEND

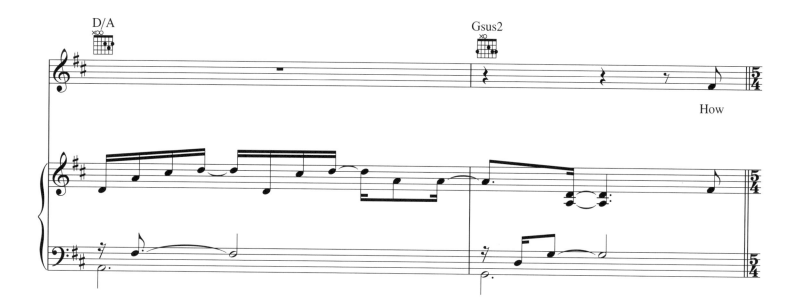

How

deep the Fa - ther's love for us; how vast be - yond all meas - ure that
hold the man up - on a cross, my sin up - on His shoul - ders. A -
will not boast in an - y - thing, no gifts, no pow'r, no wis - dom, but

He should give His on-ly Son to make a wretch His treas - ure. How
shamed, I hear my mock-ing voice call out a-mong the scoff - ers. It
I will boast in Je - sus Christ, His death and res - ur - rec - tion. Why

great the pain of sear - ing loss. The Fa - ther turns His face a - way as
was my sin that held Him there un - til it was ac - com - plished. His
should I gain from His re - ward? I can - not give an an - swer, but

wounds which mar the Cho - sen One bring man - y sons to glo -
dy - ing breath has brought me life. I know that it is fin -
this I know with all my heart: His wounds have paid my ran -

78

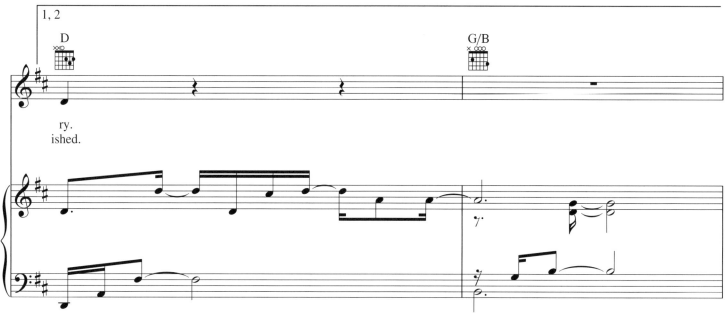

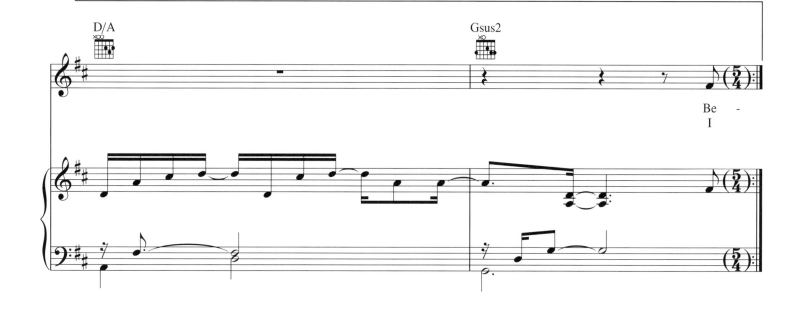

can - not give an an - swer, but this I know with all my heart: His

wounds have paid my ran - som.

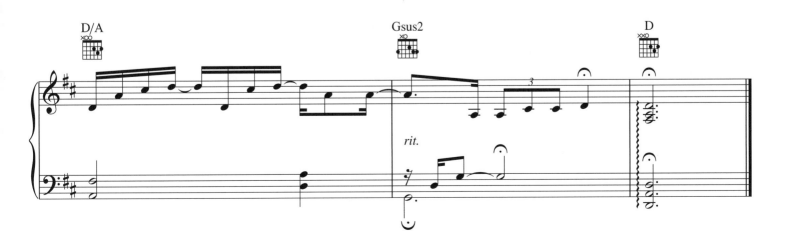

rit.

HOW GREAT IS OUR GOD

Words and Music by CHRIS TOMLIN,
JESSE REEVES and ED CASH

With praise

The splen-dor of ___ a King, ___
age to age ___ He stands, ___ and

clothed in maj - es - ty. _____ Let all the earth ___ re - joice, ___
time is in _____ His hands. ____ Be - gin - ning and ___ the End, ___

___ all the earth ___ re - joice. ___ He wraps ___ Him - self ___ in light, ___
___ Be - gin - ning and ___ the End. ___ The God - head, Three ___ in One, ___

* Recorded a half step lower.

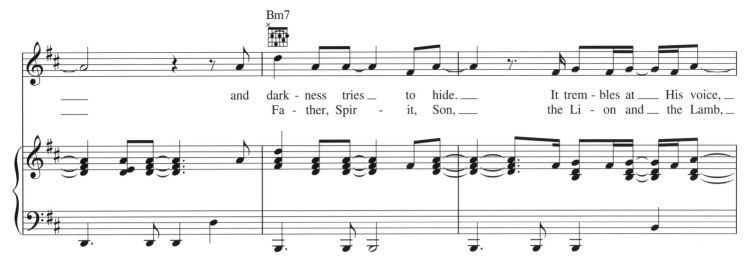

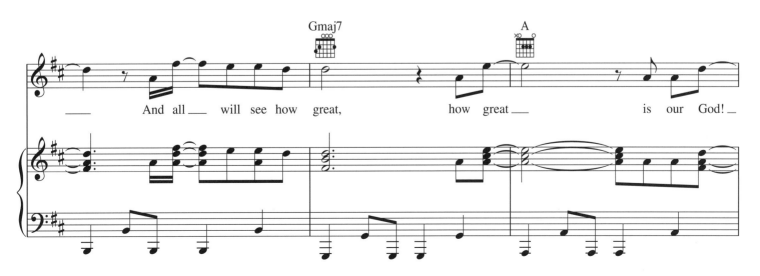

How great ____ is our God! ____

____ Sing with me: ____ How great is our God! ____

____ And all ____ will see how great, how great ____ is our God! ____

How great ____ ____

IN CHRIST ALONE

Words and Music by KEITH GETTY
and STUART TOWNEND

MAJESTY
(Here I Am)

Words and Music by MARTIN SMITH
and STUART GARRARD

Moderately slow

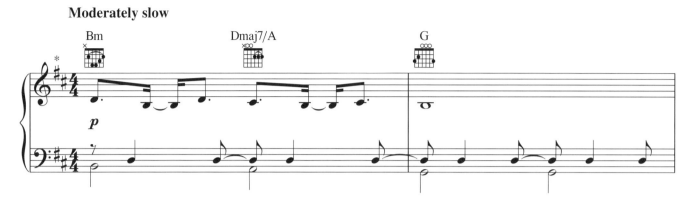

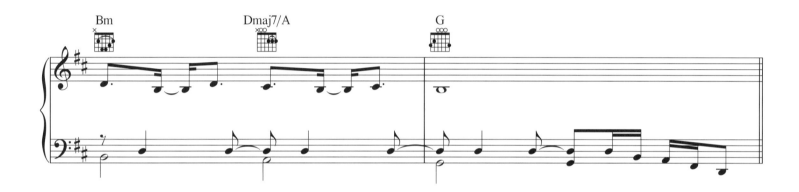

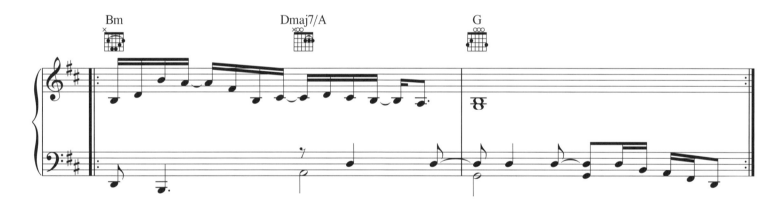

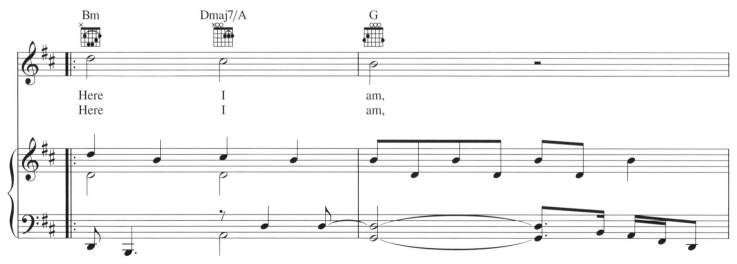

Here   I   am,
Here   I   am,

*Recorded a half step lower.

hum - bled by Your maj - es - ty, _____
hum - bled by the love that You give, _____ for -

cov - ered by Your grace so _____ free. _____
giv - en so that I can for - give. _____ So

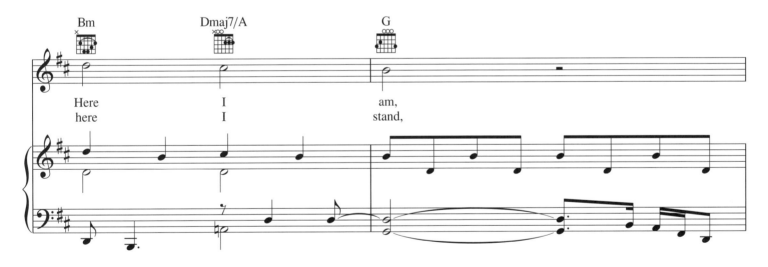

Here I am,
here I stand,

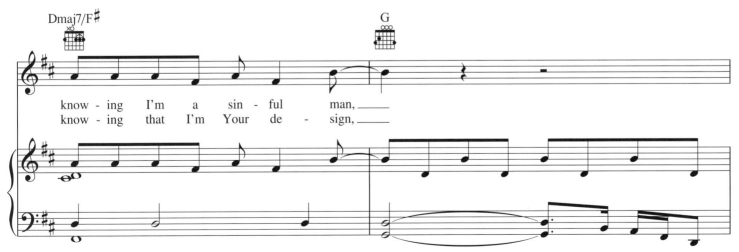

know - ing I'm a sin - ful man, _____
know - ing that I'm Your de - sign, _____

89

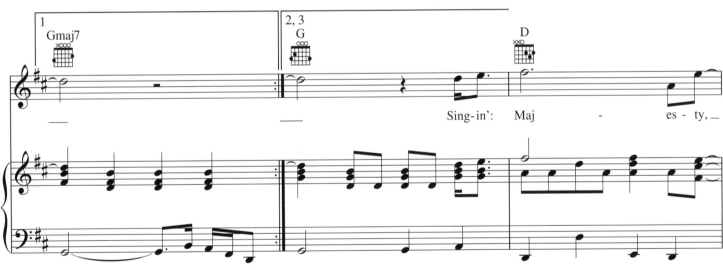

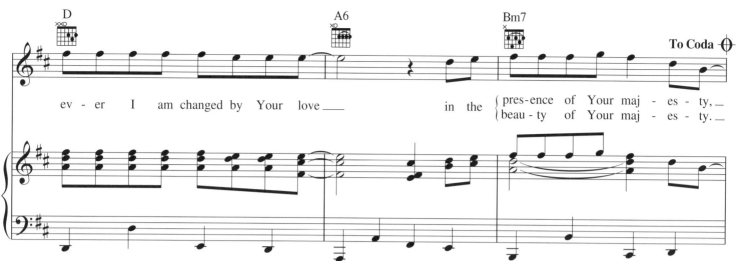

ev - er I am changed by Your love ___ in the { pres-ence of Your maj - es - ty,
{ beau-ty of Your maj - es - ty. ___

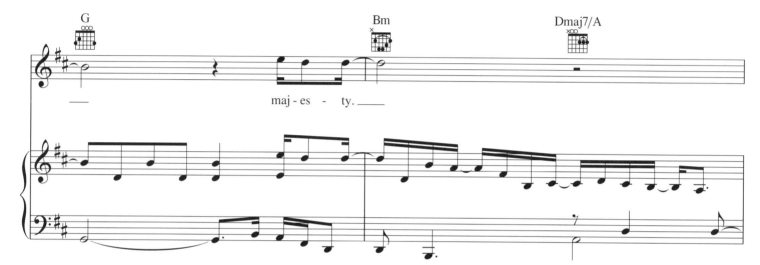

___ maj - es - ty. ___

We're sing - in':

LORD, REIGN IN ME

Words and Music by
BRENTON BROWN

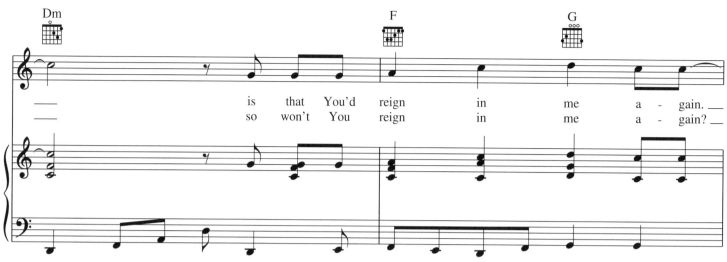

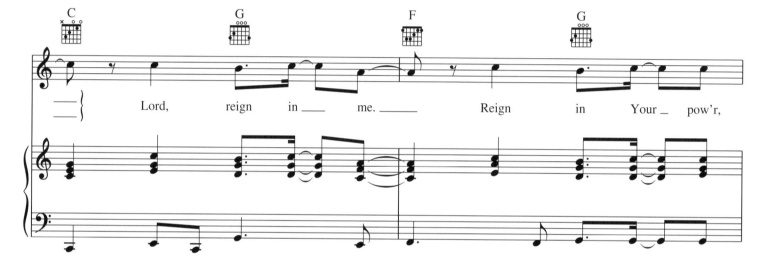

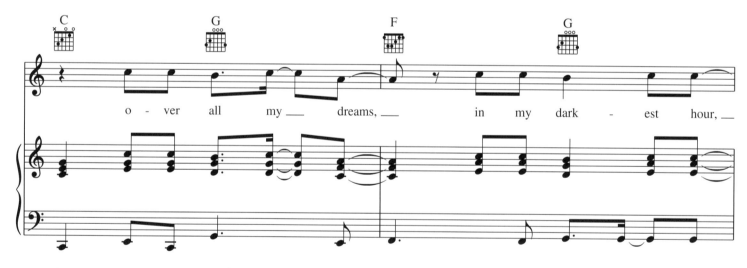

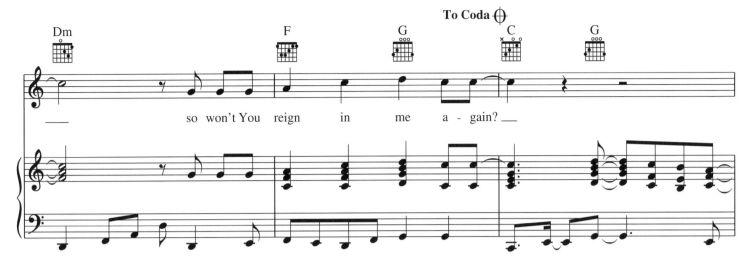

so won't You reign in me a - gain? ___

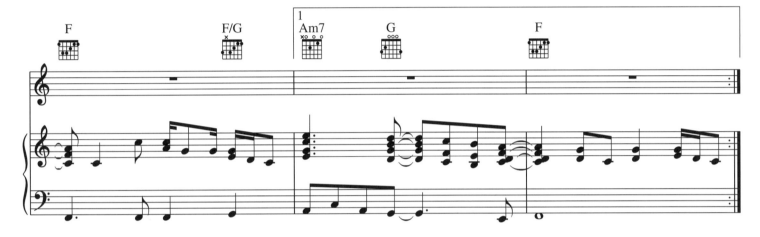

O - ver all the ___ earth ___

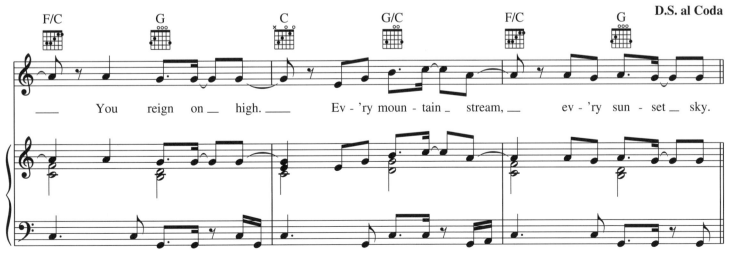

___ You reign on ___ high. ___ Ev - 'ry moun - tain ___ stream, ___ ev - 'ry sun - set ___ sky.

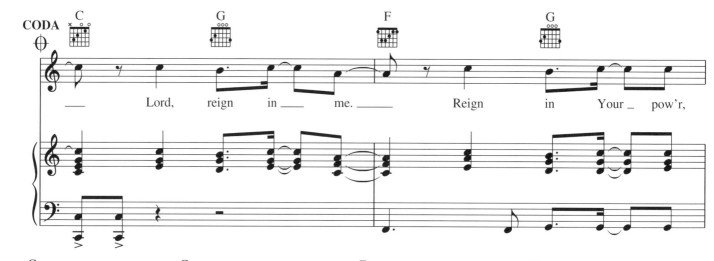

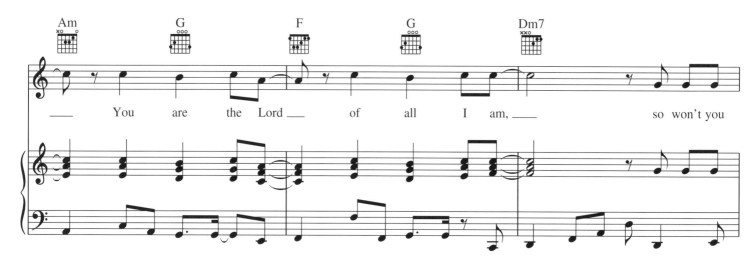

reign in me a - gain? __ Come and reign, Lord; __ won't You reign in me a - gain? __

Hey, __ yeah, __ yeah, __ yeah, __ mm. __

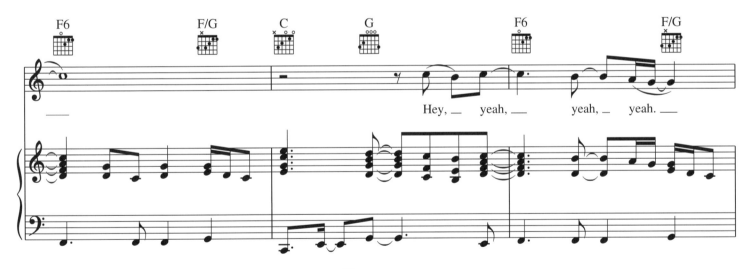

Hey, __ yeah, __ yeah, __ yeah. __

Slower

rall.

MARVELOUS LIGHT

Words and Music by
CHARLIE HALL

*Recorded a half step lower.

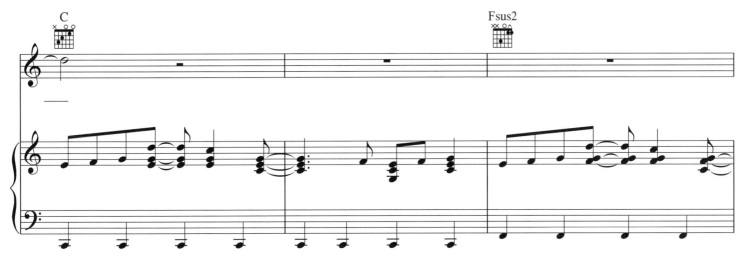

I once was

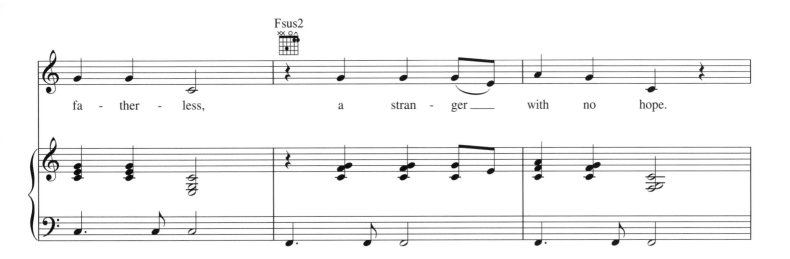

fa - ther - less, a stran - ger ____ with no hope.

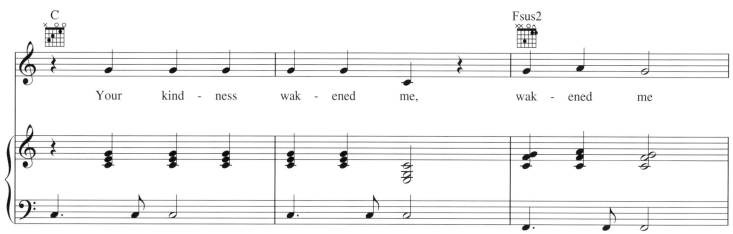

Your kind - ness wak - ened me, wak - ened me

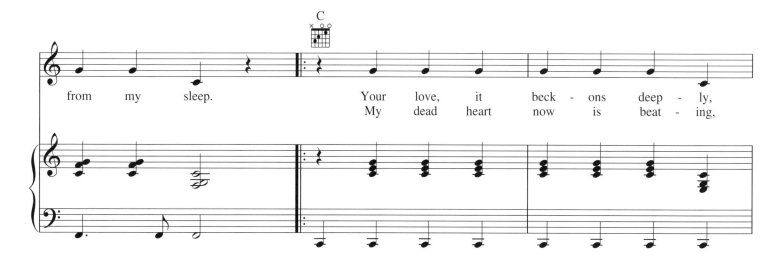

from my sleep.

Your love, it beck - ons deep - ly,
My dead heart now is beat - ing,

a call to ____ come and die.
my deep - est ____ stain's now clean.

By grace now
Your breath fills

I will come and take this life, take Your life.
up my lungs. Now I'm free, now I'm free.

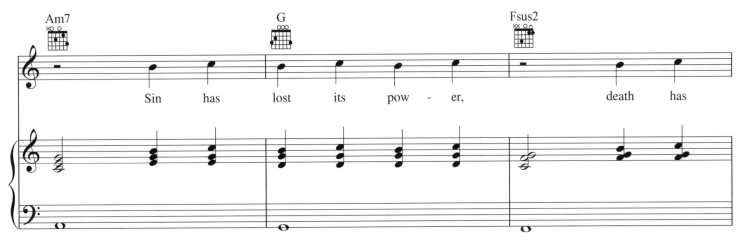

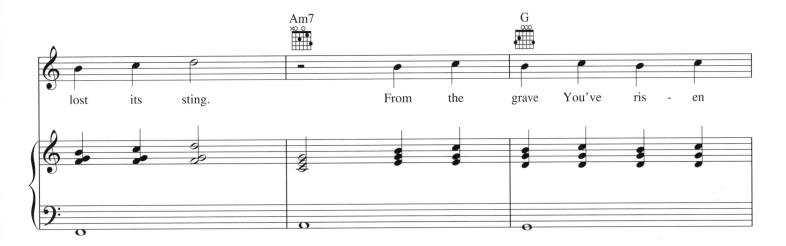

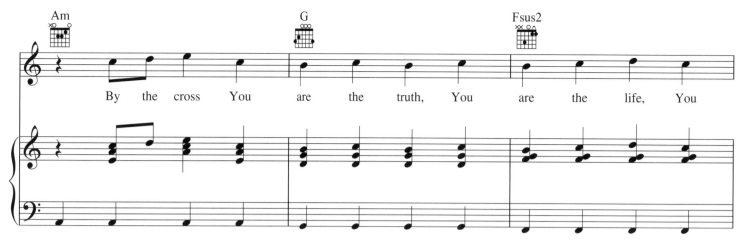

By the cross You are the truth, You are the life, You

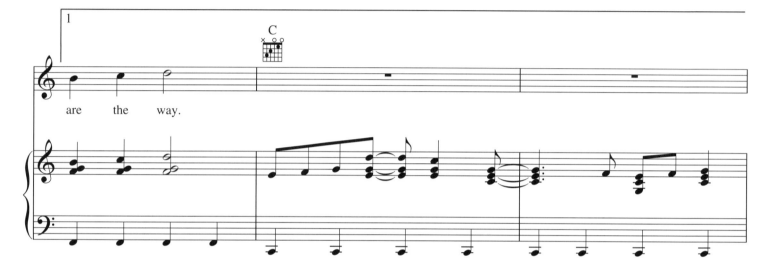

are the way.

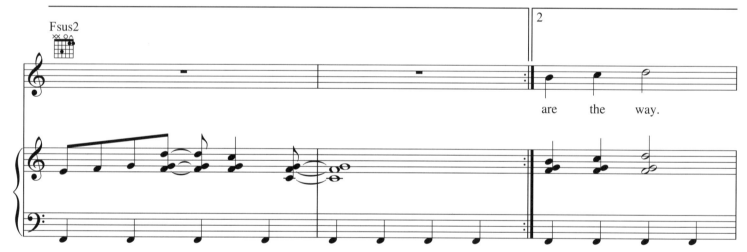

are the way.

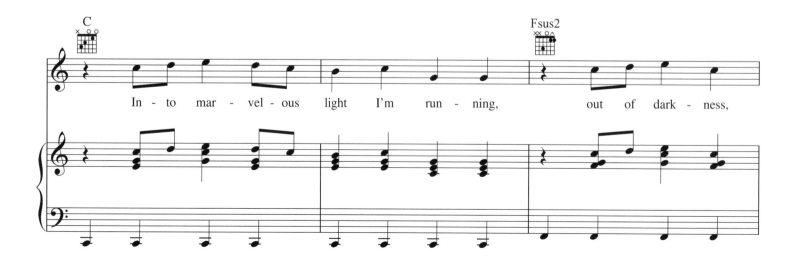

In - to mar - vel - ous light I'm run - ning, out of dark - ness,

out of shame. By the cross You are the truth, You

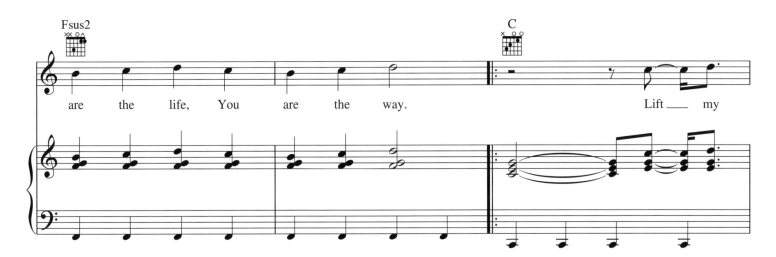

are the life, You are the way. Lift ___ my

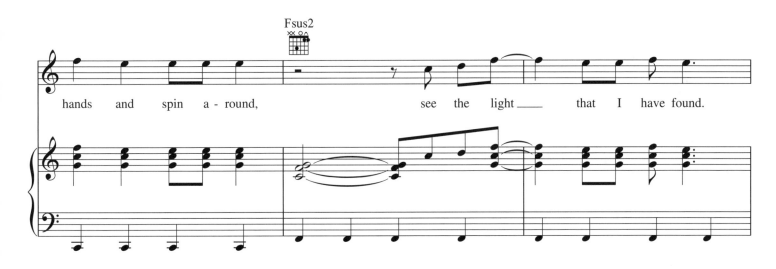

hands and spin a - round, see the light ___ that I have found.

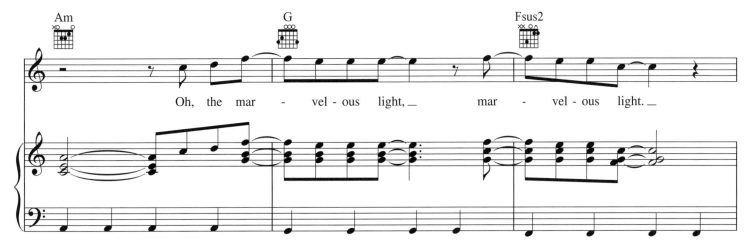

Oh, the mar - vel - ous light, ___ mar - vel - ous light. ___

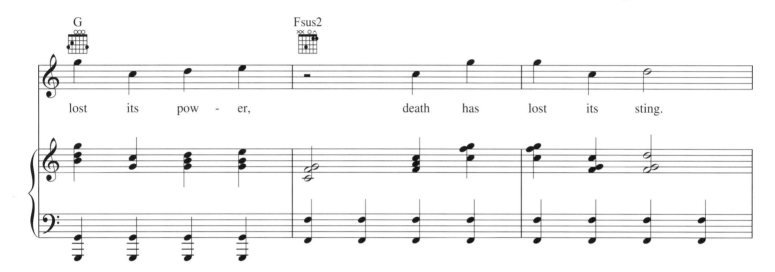

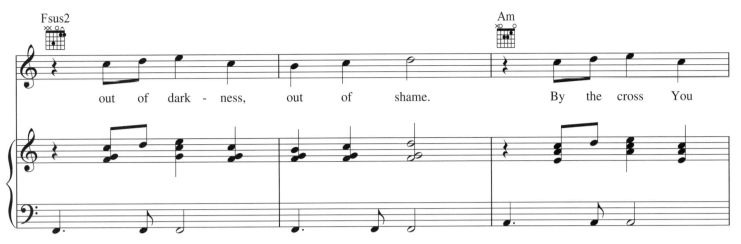

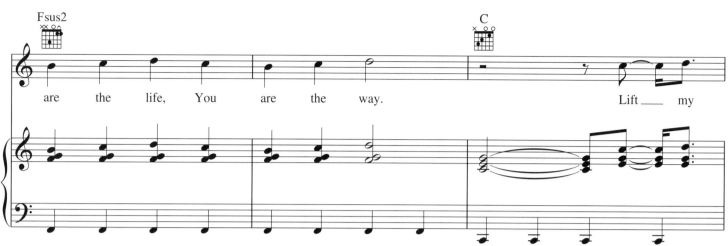

are the life, You are the way. Lift ___ my

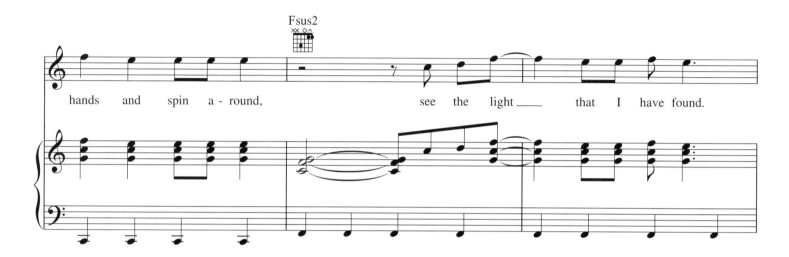

hands and spin a - round, see the light ___ that I have found.

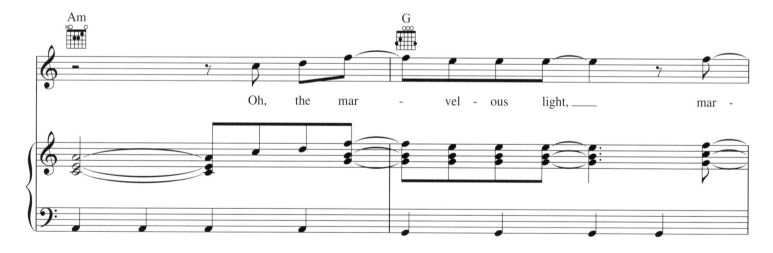

Oh, the mar - vel - ous light, ___ mar -

- vel - ous light. ___

O PRAISE HIM
(All This for a King)

Words and Music by
DAVID CROWDER

Moderately fast

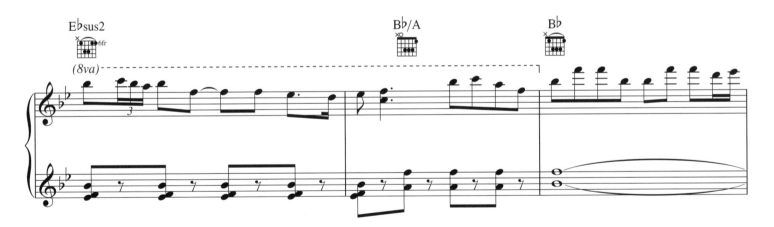

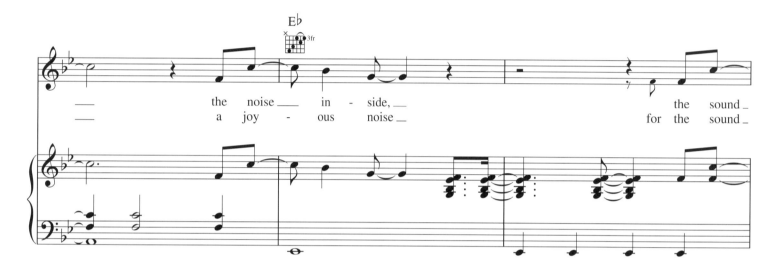

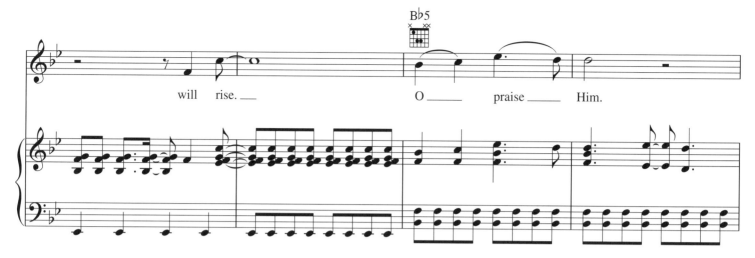

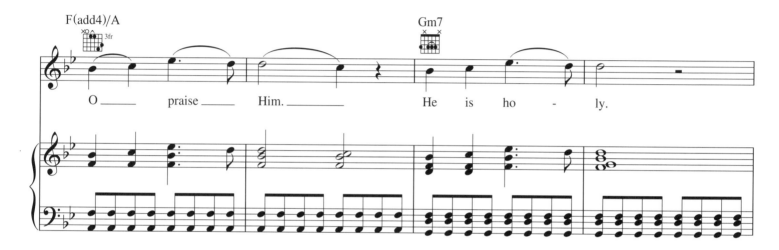

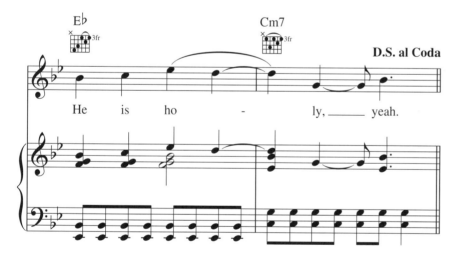

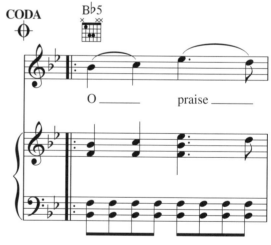

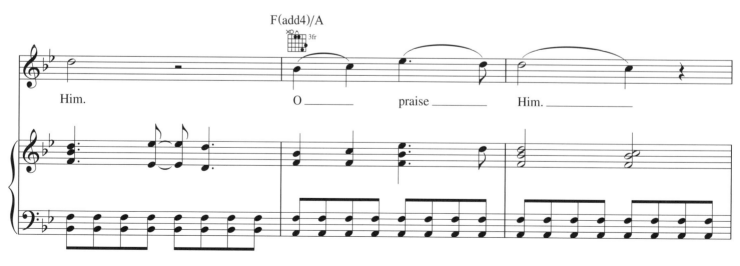

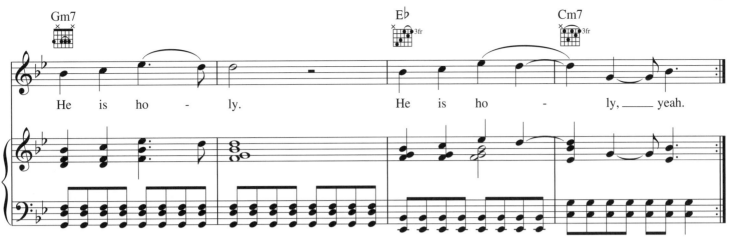

He is ho - ly. He is ho - ly, _____ yeah.

O la la _ la la la _ la. O

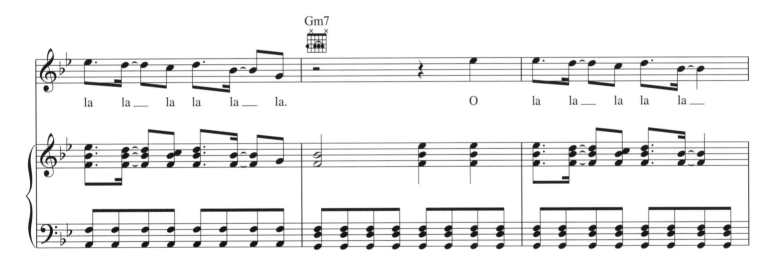

la la _ la la la _ la. O la la _ la la la _

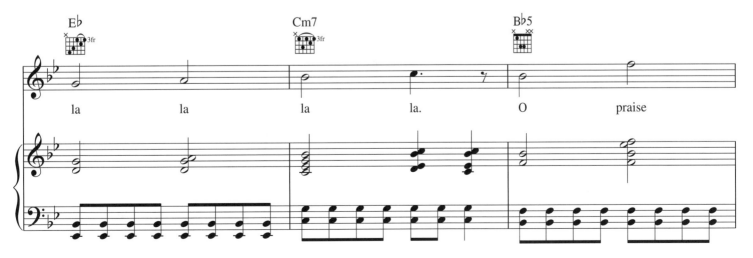

la la la la. O praise

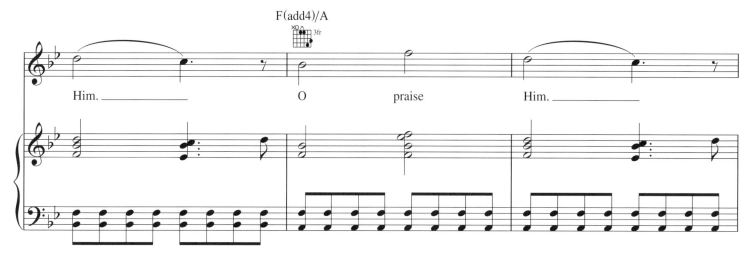

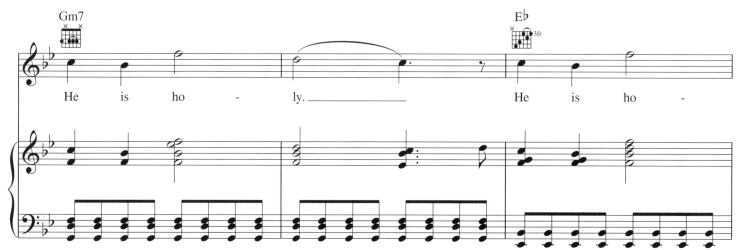

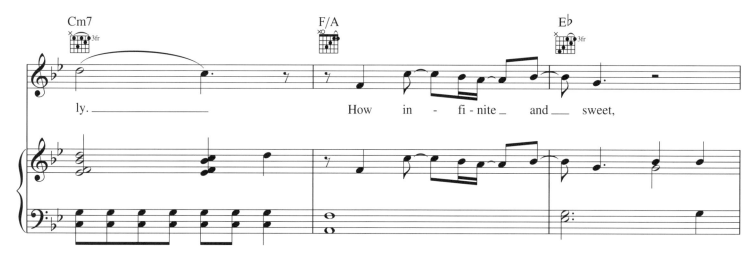

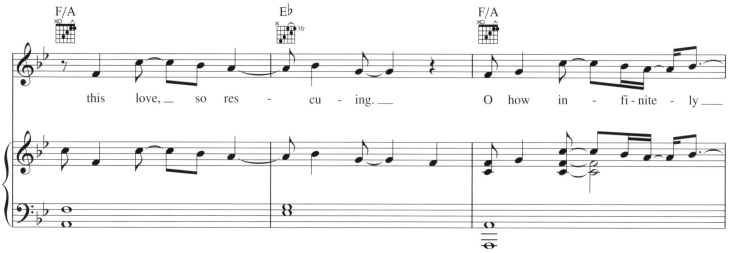

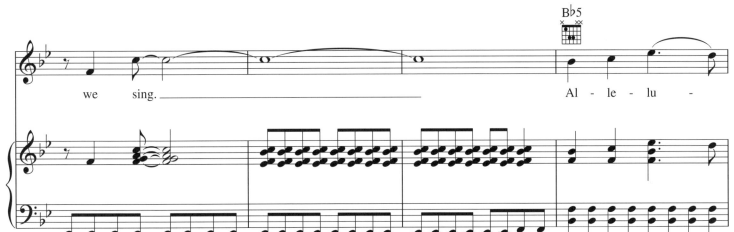

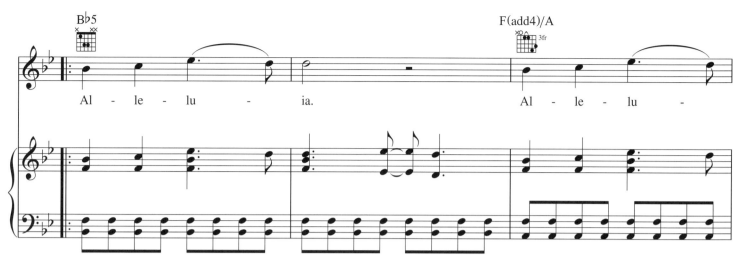

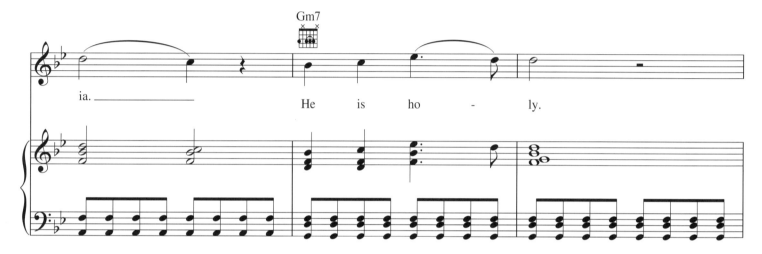

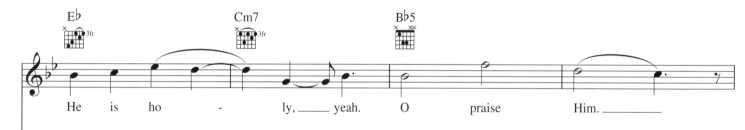

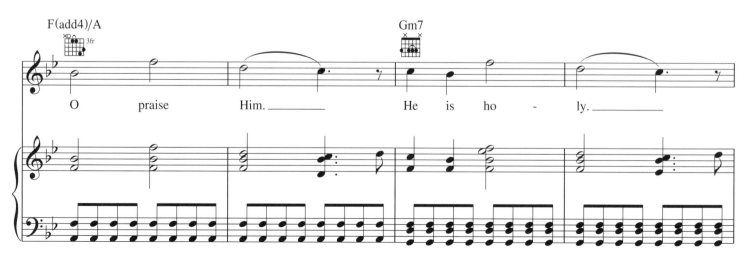

He is ho - ly. _____

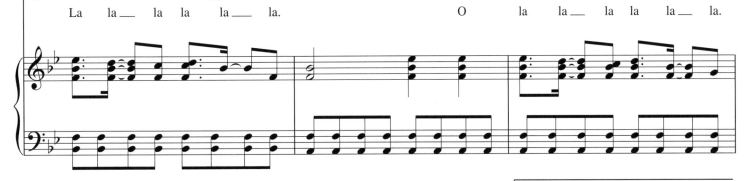

La la la la la la. O la la la la la la.

O la la la la la, la la

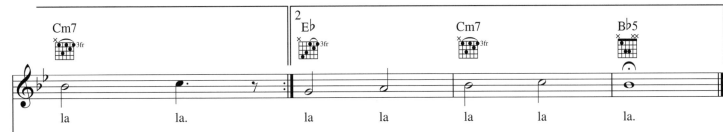

la la. la la la la la.

OUR GOD REIGNS

Words and Music by STUART GARRARD, JOHN THATCHER,
TIM JUPP, STEWART SMITH and MARTIN SMITH

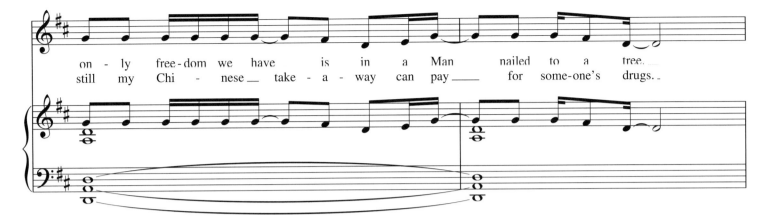

on - ly free - dom we have is in a Man nailed to a tree.
still my Chi - nese take - a - way can pay for some - one's drugs.

1

2

G

A

Our God reigns,

A   Bm   A/C#

our God reigns.   For - ev - er___ Your King - dom reigns.__

The West has found a gun _ and it's

load - ed with "un - sure." _ Nip and tuck _ if you have the bucks _ in a

race to find _ a cure. _ Psalm one hun - dred and thir - ty - nine _ is the

con - science to our self - ish crime. _ God did - n't screw up _ when He made _

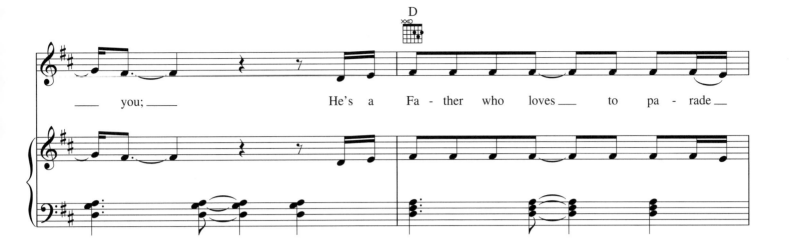

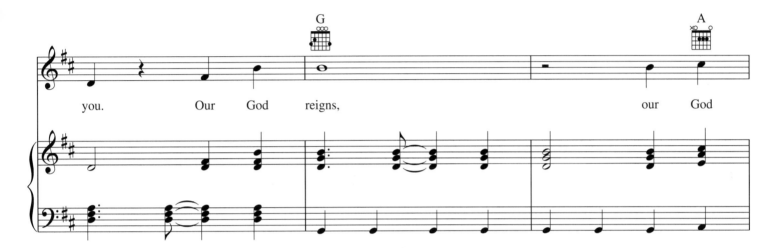

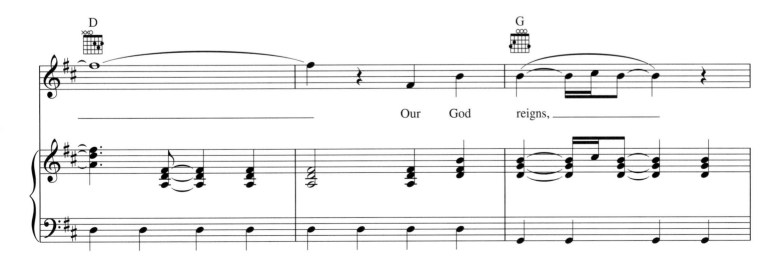

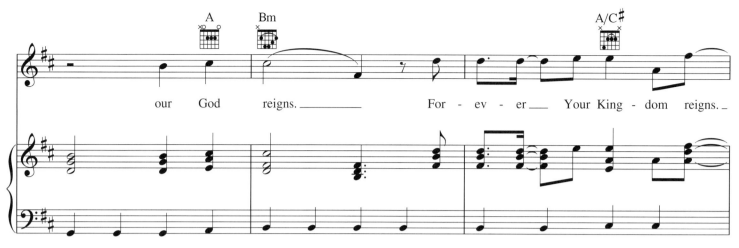

our God reigns. _____ For - ev - er ___ Your King - dom reigns. _

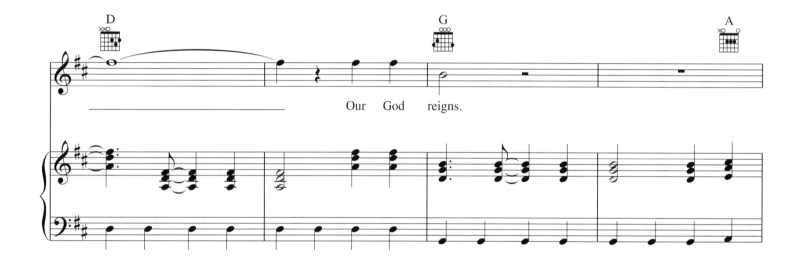

_____ Our God reigns.

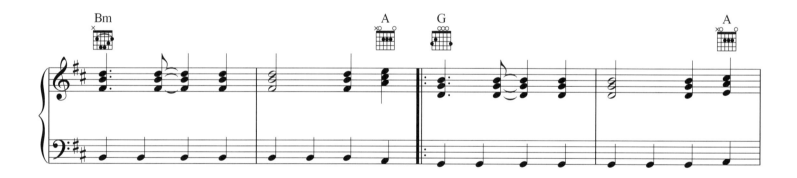

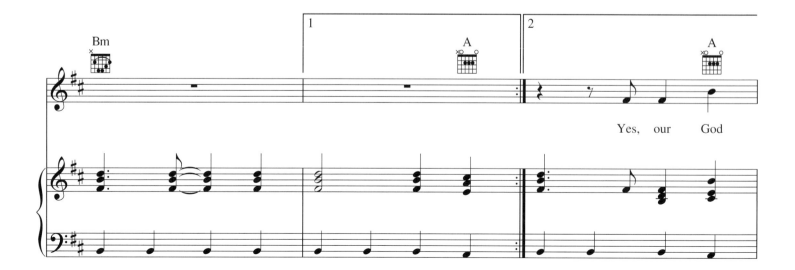

Yes, our God

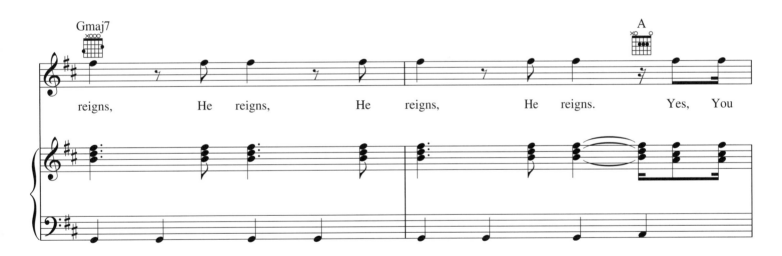

on-ly one true God, ___ but we've lost ___ the reins ___ on this world. For-

give us all, for-give us please as we fight for this bro-ken world ___ on our knees. Our God

reigns, ___ our God reigns. For-

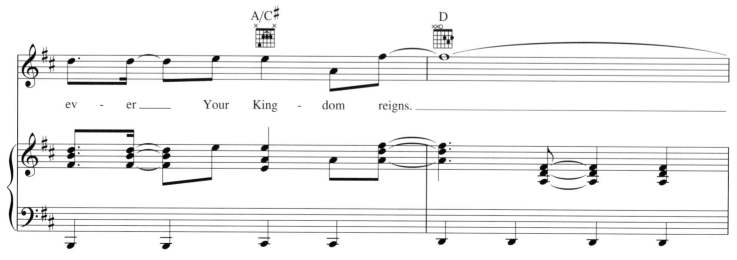

ev - er ___ Your King - dom reigns. ___

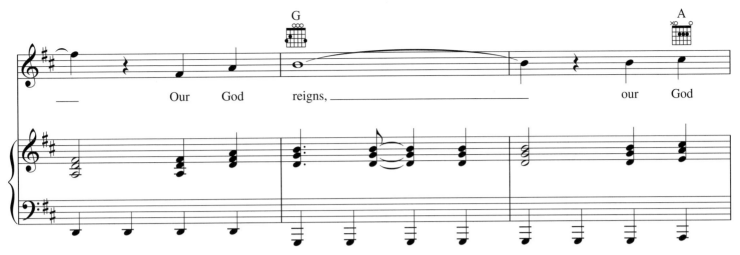

Our God reigns,_____ our God

reigns. For - ev - er___ Your King - dom reigns._____

He reigns._____ He reigns._

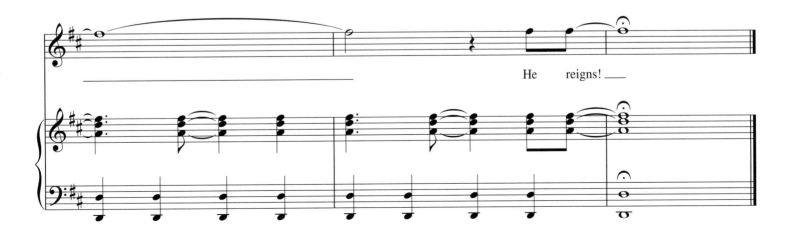

He reigns!___

SONG OF HOPE

Words and Music by ROBBIE SEAY, TAYLOR JOHNSON,
RYAN OWENS, CHASE JENKINS,
DAN HAMILTON and TEDD TJORNHOM

*Recorded a half step lower.

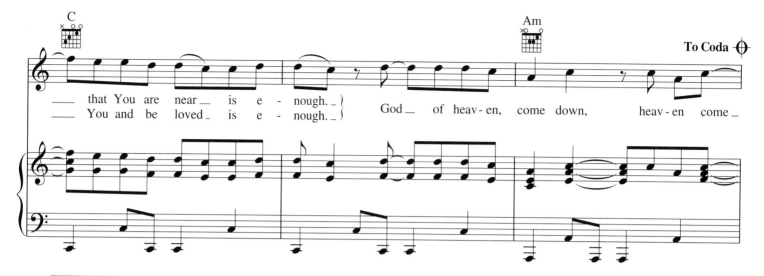

that You are near___ is e - nough.___ }
You and be loved___ is e - nough.___ }
God___ of heav - en, come down, heav - en come___

To Coda

1.
___ down, ___ yeah.

2.
___ down. ___ Oh, sing ___

D.S. al Coda

CODA

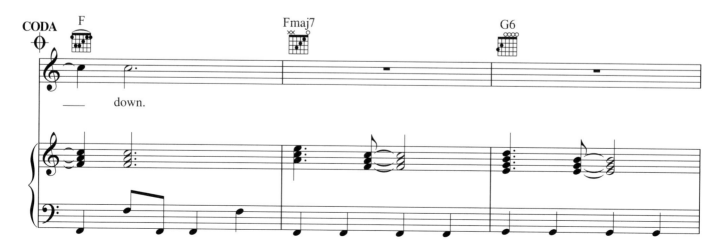

___ down.

Hal - le -

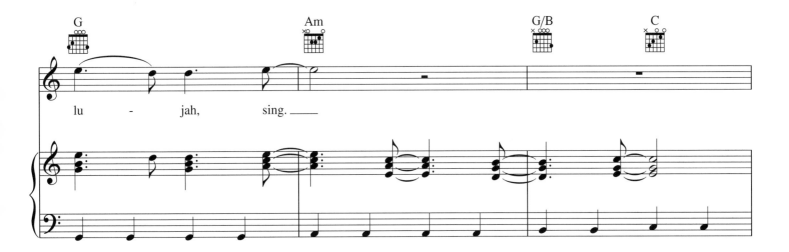

lu - jah, sing. ____

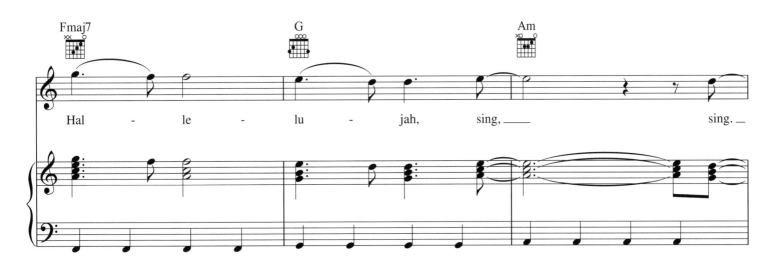

Hal - le - lu - jah, sing, ____ sing. ____

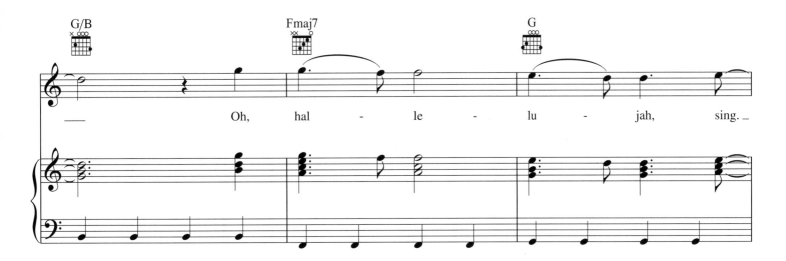

____ Oh, hal - le - lu - jah, sing. ____

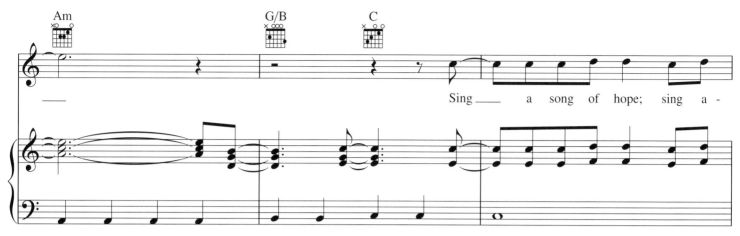

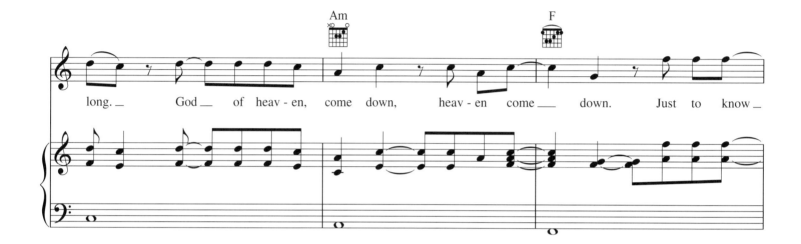

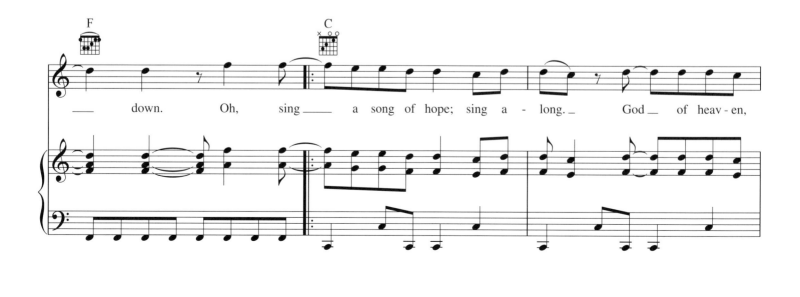

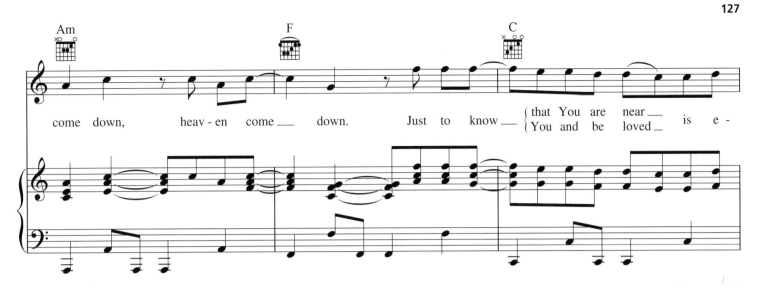

come down, heav-en come ___ down. Just to know ___ {that You are near ___ is e-
                                                    {You and be loved ___ is e-

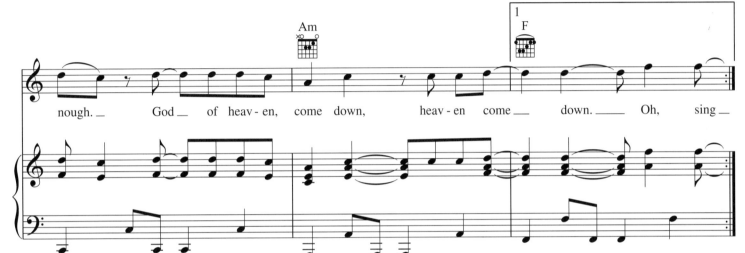

nough. ___ God ___ of heav-en, come down, heav-en come ___ down. ___ Oh, sing ___

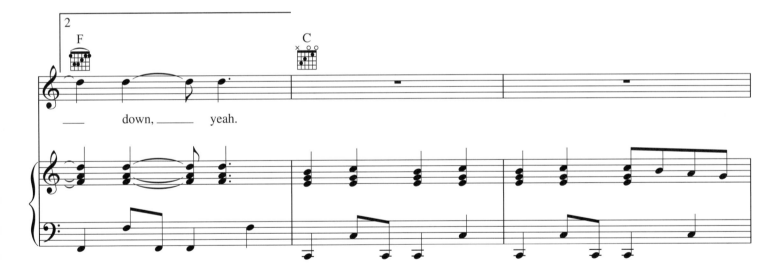

___ down, ___ yeah.

Heav-en, come ___ down.

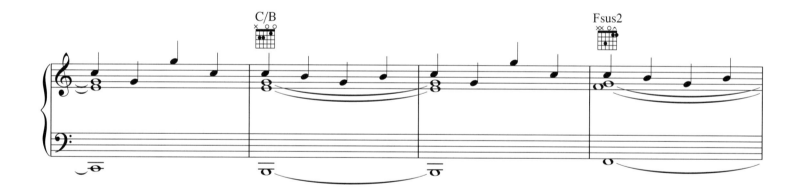

down.

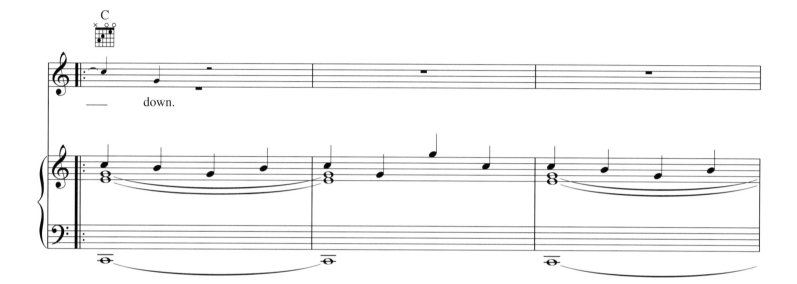

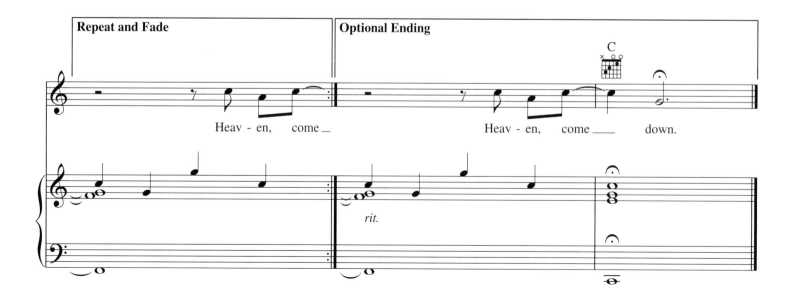

Repeat and Fade

Optional Ending

Heav - en, come ___

Heav - en, come ___ down.

rit.

YOU NEVER LET GO

Words and Music by MATT REDMAN
and BETH REDMAN

Recorded a half step lower.

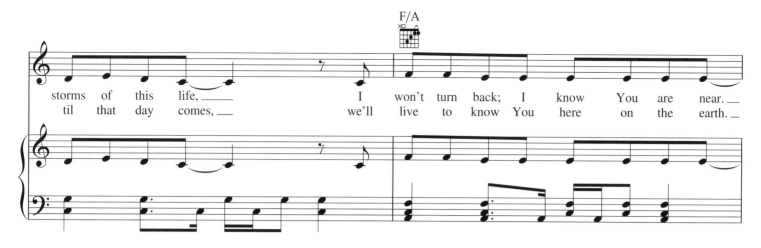

storms of this life, _____ I won't turn back; I know You are near. _____
til that day comes, _____ we'll live to know You here on the earth. _____

_____ And I will fear no e -

vil, for my God is with _____

me. And if my God is with _____

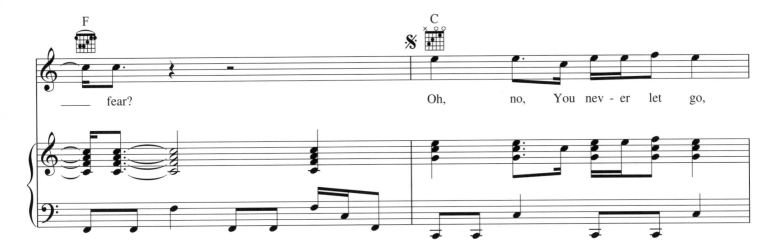

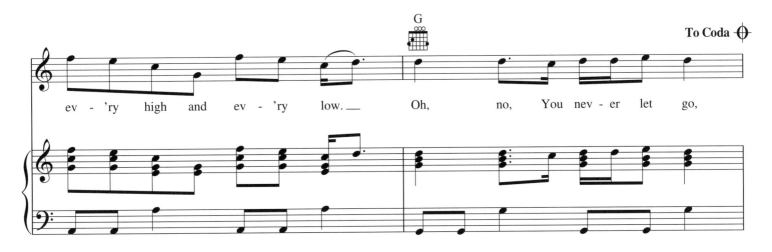

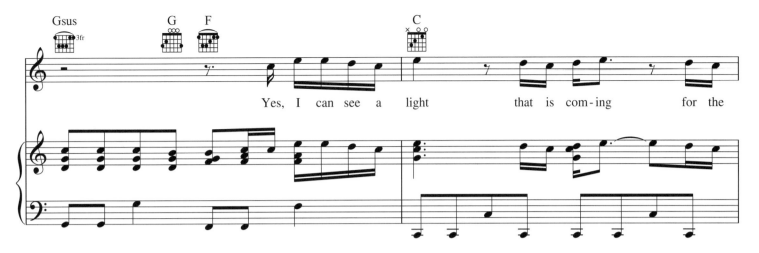

Yes, I can see a light that is com - ing for the

heart that holds on. ___ And there will be an end to these trou - bles, but un -

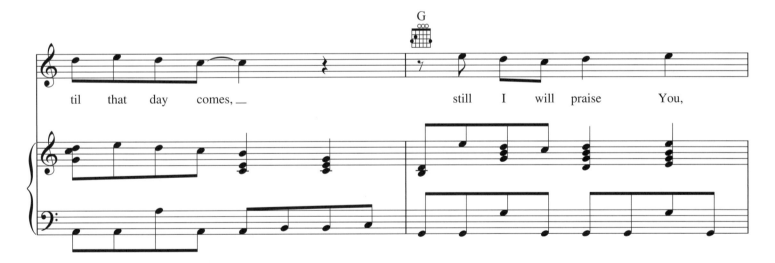

til that day comes, ___ still I will praise You,

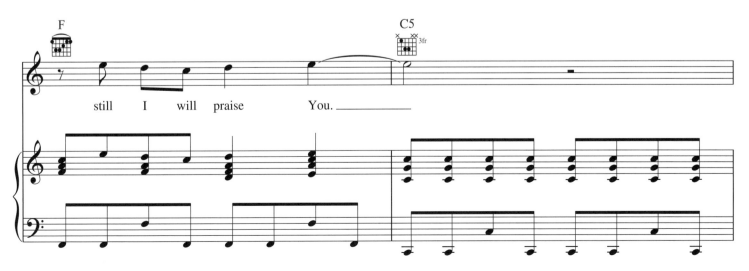

still I will praise You. ___

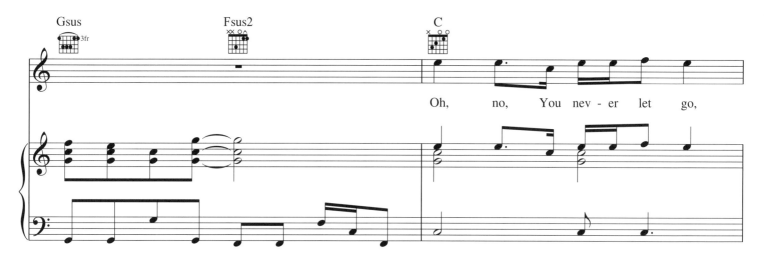

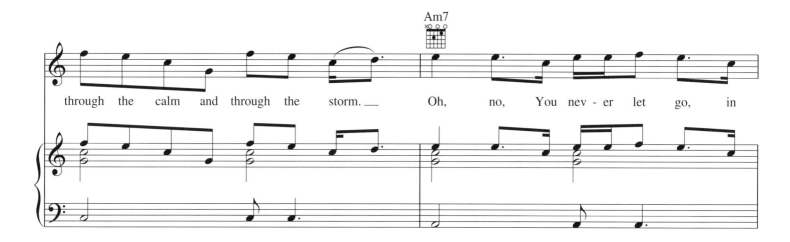

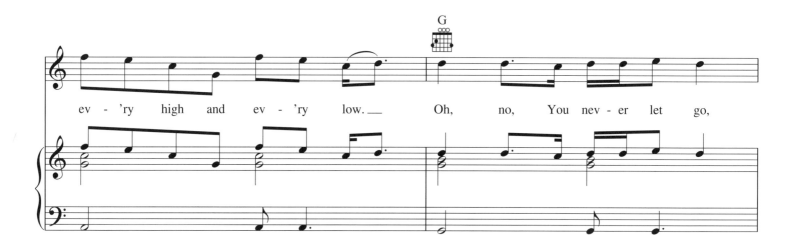

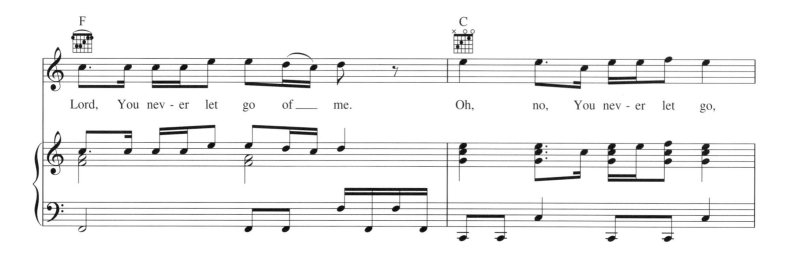

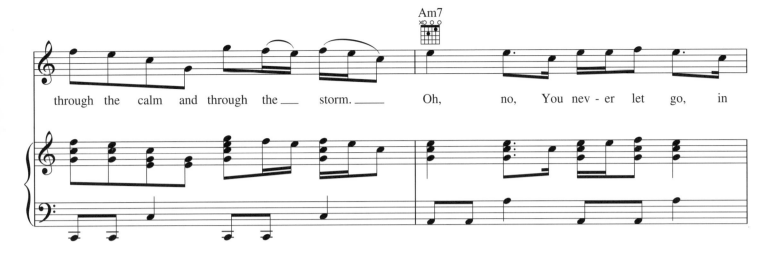

through the calm and through the ___ storm. ___ Oh, no, You nev - er let go, in

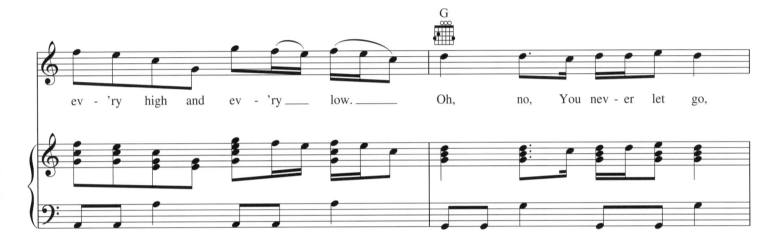

ev - 'ry high and ev - 'ry ___ low. ___ Oh, no, You nev - er let go,

Lord, You nev - er let go of ___ me. ___

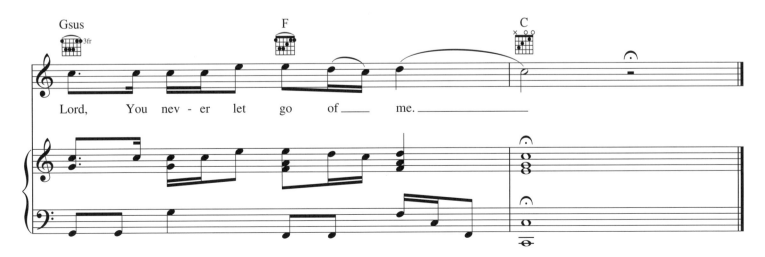

Lord, You nev - er let go of ___ me. ___

WE FALL DOWN

Words and Music by
CHRIS TOMLIN

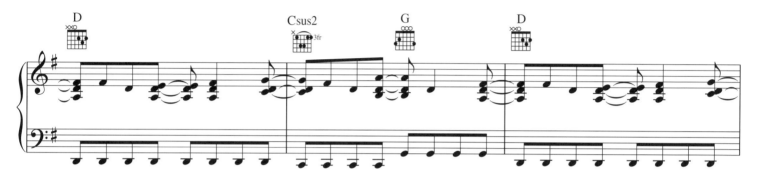

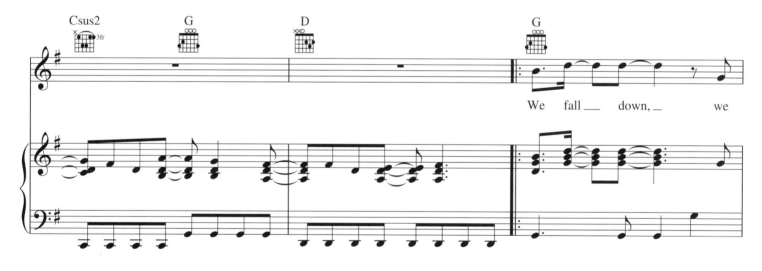

We fall __ down, __ we

lay our __ crowns __ at the feet _____ of Je - sus. The

*Recorded a half step lower.

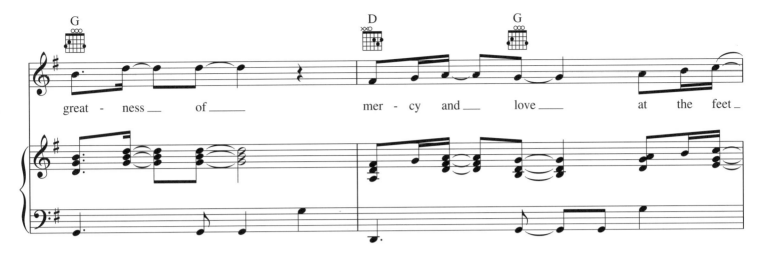

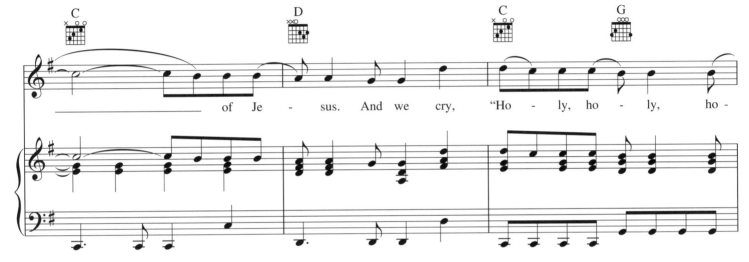

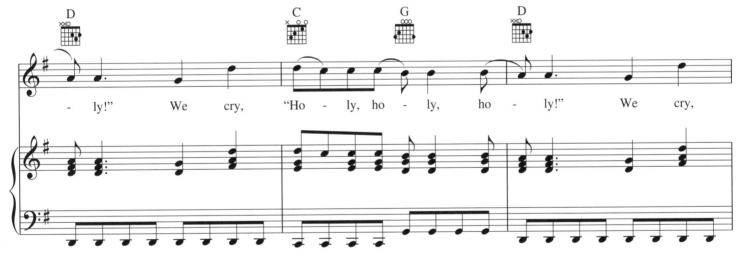

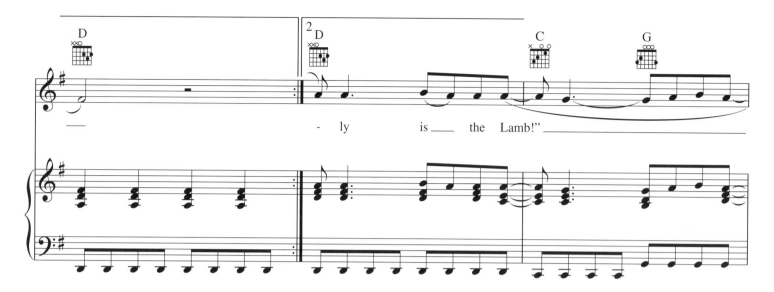

-ly   is___   the Lamb!"_____

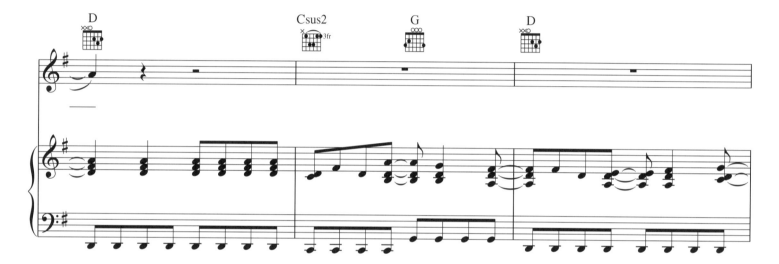

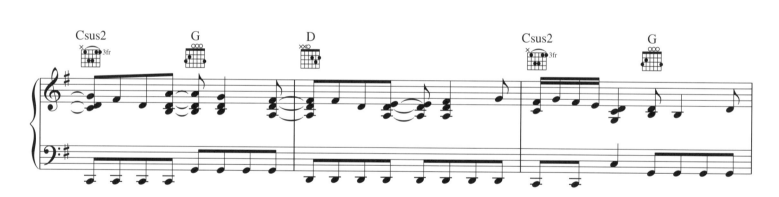

And we   cry,

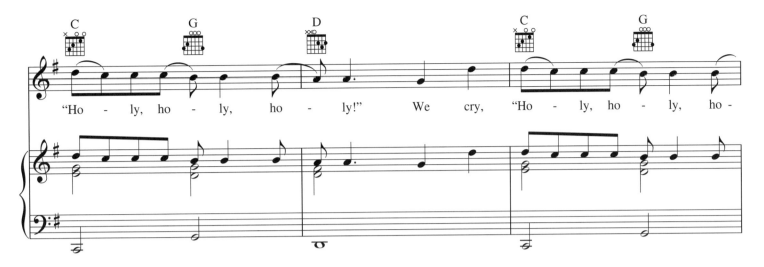

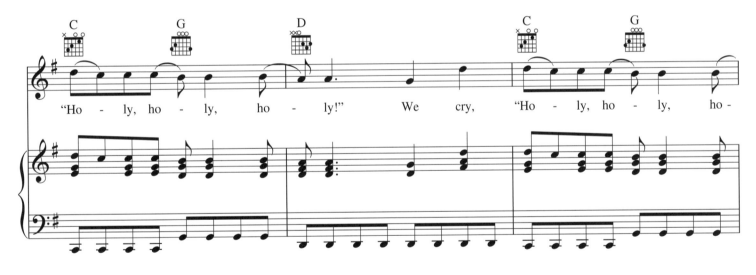

YOU ARE MY KING
(Amazing Love)

Words and Music by
BILLY JAMES FOOTE

With praise

I'm for-giv-en be-cause You were for-sak - en.

I'm ac-cept - ed, _____ You were con - demned. _

I'm a - live ___ and well; _ Your Spir - it is with - in ___ me be -

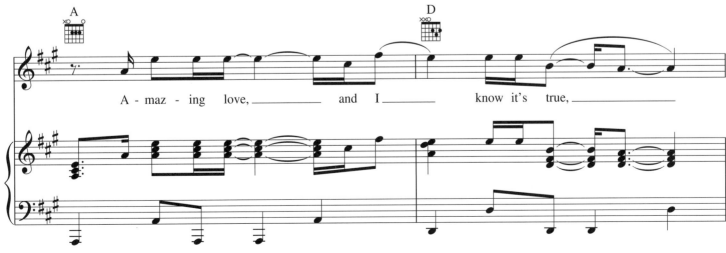

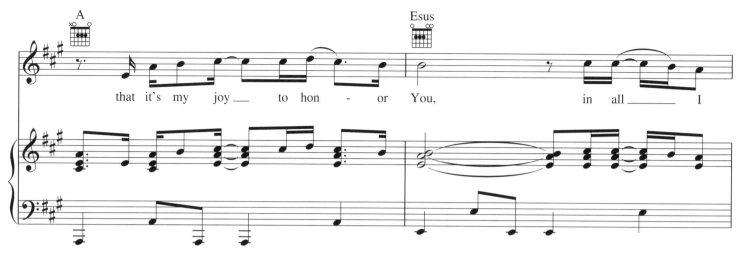

that it's my joy ___ to hon - or You, in all ___ I

do to hon - or You.

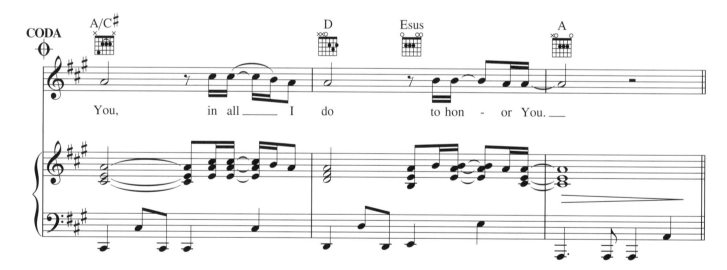

You, in all ___ I do to hon - or You. ___

You are my ___ King, You are my ___

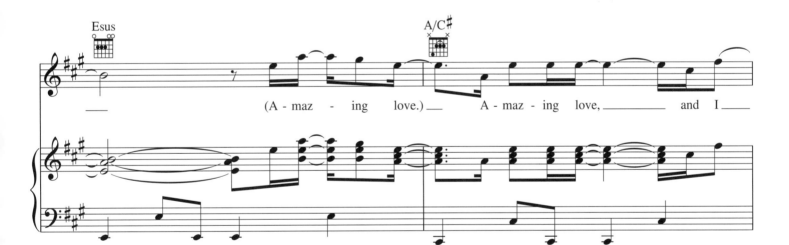

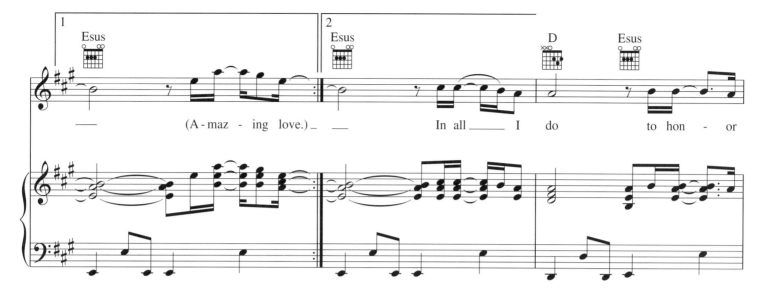

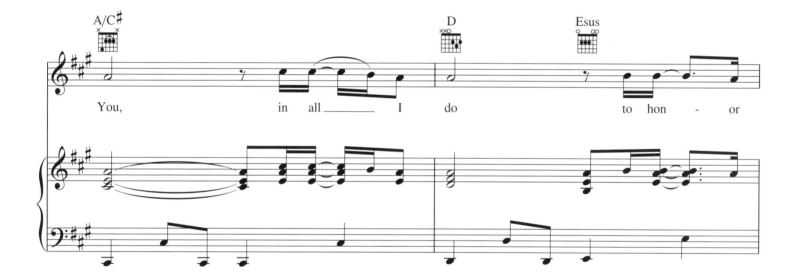

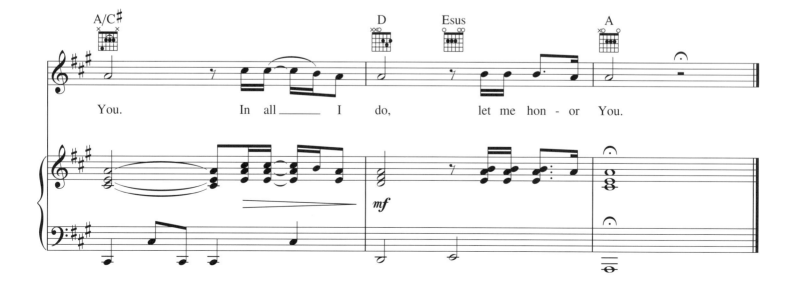